Jo Newman 08.

Kant On Moral Practice

Kant On
Moral Practice

A Study of Moral Success and Failure

by
Rex Patrick Stevens

Mercer University Press
Macon, Ga. 31207

To the memory of Phillip

"When a man prides himself on being able to understand and interpret
the books of Chrysippus, say to yourself, 'If Chrysippus had not written obscurely this man would have had nothing on which to pride himself'."

—Epictetus

Library of Congress Cataloging in Publication Data
Stevens, Rex Patrick, 1942-
Kant on moral practice.
Bibliography: p. 171.
Includes index.
1. Kant, Immanuel, 1742-1804—Ethics.
2. Ethics. I. Title.
B2799.E8S72   170'.92'4   81-9489
ISBN 0-86554-012-8   AACR2

Acknowledgements

I cannot adequately express my gratitude to my mentor, Steven Schwarzschild, for his patience and help over the past several years. Though he is not responsible for the content of this work, without his strong sense of what is important in Kant's texts, my study would have been an intellectual nightmare.

There are two very special people whose concerns for my work and being appear throughout the text of my study. There is no better friend than Garnet Jex whose hours of patient listening allowed many of the sections to coalesce in my mind. He is the person for whom I have most wanted this study to be honest and readable. Also, Angel Medina has given me many hours of intellectual advice and proofreading time. To him I owe many of the central conceptions of my study. His influence on this study is immense. I thank both Garnet and Angel for their generosity.

I could not have completed this work without the help of several people: Dean Thomas Trimble of Mercer University, who supported my work with grants and with a release from my teaching duties for one school term; Mrs. Livonia Howard, who prepared the original typescript of this manuscript; and Mrs. Doris Wilder, who fretted with me through the final drafts of the manuscript and who taught the Burroughs "Redactor II" a few lessons about the place of word-processors in human life. To these three people I owe a debt of gratitude.

Without the support of my family, Jane, Eric, and David, I would not have understood the necessity of connecting philosophical issues with the great concerns of everyday life. That is what is most important to me. I thank them for everything.

Rex Stevens
June 1981

Note on Kant's
German Texts
and Translations

Throughout this essay, translations of Kant's works which are available to English readers have been used. The notes often supply the original German of certain crucial passages. All research in the German texts has been done in Ernst Cassirer's edition of Kant's collected works. It is to this edition of Kant's work that the citations refer:

> *Immanuel Kants Werke.* Edited by Ernst Cassirer. Eleven volumes. Berlin: Bruno Cassirer, 1912-1922.

All references in the footnotes are to Cassirer's edition. Titles are abbreviated and are followed by the volume and page number(s), the translator's last name, and page number(s) of the translation. (A comprehensive list of English translations of Kant's work is made available in the Selected Bibliography.) For example:

[135] *Religion*, 6:324; Greene, p. 162.

refers to the title abbreviated *Religion* which is in volume 6 of the

Cassirer collection and in Greene's translation. So the reference is to page 324 of volume 6 of the original, and to page 162 of the translation.

For convenience, a list of abbreviated titles used in the notes, along with the translator's last name, follows:

Anthropologie = *Anthropologie in pragmatische Hinsicht*; Gregor.

Aufklärung = *Beantwortung der Frage: Was ist Aufklärung?*; Beck.

Beginnings = *Mutmasslicher Anfang der Menschengeschichte*; Beck (in *On History*).

Ende = *Das Ende aller Dinge*; Beck (in *On History*).

Grundlegung or *Groundwork* (in text) = *Grundlegung zur Metaphysic der Sitten*; Beck.

Idea = *Idee zu einer allgemeinen Geschichte in weltbügerlicher Absicht*; Beck (in *On History*).

K1 or first *Critique* (in text) = *Kritik der reinen Vernunft*; Smith.

KPR or second *Critique* (in text) = *Kritik der praktischer Vernunft*; Beck.

K3 or third *Critique* (in text) = *Kritik der Urteilskraft*; Meredith.

Logik = *Vorlesungen über Logik*; Hartman.

Perpetual Peace = *Zum ewigen Frieden: Ein philosophischen Entwurf*; Beck (in *On History*).

Religion = *Die Religion innerhalb der Grenzen der blossen Vernunft*; Greene.

Theodicee = *Über das Misslingen aller philosophischen Versuche in der Theodicee*; Despland (in *Kant on History and Religion*).

Theorie und Praxis = *Über den Gemeinspruch: Das mag in der Theorie richtig sein, taugt aber nicht für die Praxis*; Ashton.

Tugendlehre = *Metaphysik der Sitten in zwei Teiler*; Ellington.

Table of Contents

Introduction

The aim of this study is to present a reinterpretation of Kant's moral philosophy. This reinterpretation differs from numerous others in its primary emphasis upon the subjectively practical aspects of Kant's moral theory. The purpose is to examine several of Kant's familiar works, especially the *Groundwork*, from the point of view of one who has surveyed Kantian territories which are not well known by most philosophers who are acquainted primarily with Kant's critical works and with his formal philosophical doctrines.

The thesis of this study is that Kant's late popular essays make explicit a background against which the formal moral doctrines can be more easily interpreted. It is in the late essays on history, religion and anthropology that Kant's conception of the good will is revealed along with all of its implications. It is clear from these late writings that the conception of the good will develops into a full-blown conception of moral dispositions. The notion of dispositions as central to morality follows from the idea that the good will is really an attitude of sorts adopted by the moral agent as a morally practical posture vis-à-vis himself and others. Kant's view is, then, that actions gain what moral worth they have by virtue of being animated by—preconditioned by—

moral dispositions. These dispositions are created and maintained by the agent himself. They are inseparable from a set of convictions to which the agent is freely committed.

It is not just that morality has a strong attitudinal component for Kant. From the subjectively practical standpoint morality just *is* attitudinal or dispositional. Thus the major concern of Kant is to describe these attitudes or dispositions, and to explain how they are created and maintained by moral agents. Kant shows, especially in his late works, how moral dispositions are first created, and how they are subsequently monitored and maintained. He also shows how they are corrupted and describes in great detail how certain types of character represent moral failure.

The morality of an agent depends entirely upon the extent to which he is able to purify the grounds of his own conduct; the extent to which he is successful in revolutionizing his dispositions; and, therefore, the extent to which he is able to establish for himself what Kant calls "character." What is clear from Kant's texts is that the establishment of character is no mean achievement. Many people apparently do not succeed at all in this. This study argues that Kant has presented a typology of moral failure, and that moral failure for Kant is inseparably linked to defective character. For Kant, character is defined as a way of thinking rather than a way of acting. Moral failure is, therefore, always the function of different "pathological ways of thinking."

Throughout this study several descriptions are presented of ways of thinking which Kant himself shows to be morally impoverished. Each way of thinking is pathological in the sense that it is imprisoned within the confines of identifiable *natural habits*. Each is, accordingly, a way of thinking either improperly informed by the moral law or uninformed by it altogether. Ways of thinking inattentive to the moral law begin quite naturally and gradually assume a rigidity which causes the life of the agent to crystallize into a series or a system of routines. If a routine is the crystallization of certain ways of thought (and eventually ways of acting), it is also the loss of the spontaneity which is the central feature of a life lived for the sake of moral laws. If a life is routinized, it is necessarily unfree. If it is unfree, it cannot be moral. Morality, for Kant, is freedom under laws. Where there is no freedom there is no morality either.

One discovery of this study that is of both interest and significance for Kant scholarship is that Kant has sharply differentiated between moral and non-moral attitudes by demonstrating that the former are *never habitual*, the latter *always are*. This study attempts to show what this means in concrete terms. Moral practices have, it is suggested, two things in common: (1) they are informed by the moral law, and (2) they are efforts either to destroy or to master natural habits.

Moral living is difficult not so much because we are unable to know what is right and what is wrong, but because even when we do know what is right and what is wrong, we must struggle to destroy or to master habits which erode our moral will and which make doing what we know to be right difficult. The problem, as Kant sees it, is that the effort to live morally, to struggle against habits, cannot itself become habitual. Another problem is that habits are hard to destroy or to master. Anyone who has ever tried to stop smoking knows this to be true. It is not simply that not smoking is difficult. To succeed at not smoking, for example (a minor one, I suppose), requires not only the knowledge that smoking is bad and the initial resolve to quit, but also a revolutionized view of oneself that is more difficult to manage given one's sedimented (habitual) view of oneself as a smoker. It is much easier for a smoker to think of himself as a smoker than to think of himself as a non-smoker. The reason for this is quite clear. The empirical evidence that he is a smoker is non-controvertible; the empirical evidence that he is not is simply non-existent.

Similarly, thinking of oneself and others from a moral point of view—that is, thinking of oneself and others as free to obey the moral law—is much more difficult than thinking of oneself and others as necessarily imprisoned in various determinisms. The reason for this is equally clear. We are naturally acquainted with our own weaknesses and our own faults, just as we are naturally acquainted with others' shortcomings. It is easier to take a dim view of ourselves and others than it is to take a moral view of ourselves and others. Our natural habits of thought are against us from the start. Unless we are gloriously innocent we *naturally* suspect the worst of others. We look for incriminating motivations beneath publicly charitable acts, for example. We know genuine altruism to be a rare thing. The empirical evidence seems always to reveal some secret incentive, some tax break, some advantage which makes the imputation of moral motivation almost laughable.

It is therefore much easier for us to convince ourselves of the fact that we are not free, really, to be moral, since nature is so obviously antagonistic to morality from the start. Empirically conditioned attitudes about ourselves and others are easy to assume simply because they are so naturally assumable. And they are also, as Kant pictures them, the most difficult to destroy or to manage. They become, in Kant's language, a sort of "second nature." They are habitual. Moral attitudes are not natural. They must be self-created and then constantly maintained. They are difficult to adopt and even more difficult to maintain. They are constantly endangered, according to Kant, by two powers: by human frailty, and by radical evil. The first is simply weakness of will produced by the constant bombardment of our moral ideals by the sights and sounds of human suffering, both our own and others'. The second is a natural tendency for us to deny in countless ways our own freedom and the freedom of others. The first, we might say, is nature finding excuses for our moral failures; the second, nature seeing to it that we make excuses for ourselves. Radical evil is the tendency we have to lie to ourselves about our duties, the disposition to disobey the moral law. We constantly undermine our own moral convictions in countless ways.

So the thesis of the present study in its most developed form is this: Kantian morality can be seen, when looked at from the perspective of its commonplace applications and descriptions, as the discipline of maintaining a non-natural attitude toward oneself and others. This attitude is the product of the consciousness of the moral law and is maintained by the rational construction of the ideal of a moral world in which persons are radically free from the habits of nature, free to realize moral principles in a world which is naturally void of them. The maintenance of moral attitudes is an effort supplemented by incentives which appear in the life of a moral agent as rationally produced feelings, the most important of which Kant calls "respect."

This study progresses through five chapters. The first chapter discusses Kant's notion of "common human reason," in order to capture an image of ordinary moral consciousness and the different ways it can be corrupted. In chapter two Kant's ideas about how ordinary moral consciousness can be stabilized by a process of criticism are considered. Chapter three is an intricate, even serpentine, exploration of Kant's conceptions of moral judgment and discipline.

Chapter four is an investigation into Kant's notion of the "revolution" in the ground of a person's way of thinking. This notion of revolution is connected with concrete descriptions of different courses of life. Chapter five is an imaginative construction of a moral biography, the point of which is to show, biographically, the gradual "insinuation" of reason into a moral person's way of thinking.

This study moves gradually from descriptions of various kinds of conscious states toward the conception of moral life as the totalization of these states, and as the reflective ground in which the various episodes of life are unified. Kant's moral philosophy, this study hopes to show, is not merely theoretical. Indeed it is, as Plato's was, a philosophy of life.

Note on the Literature

One who attempts a study of Kant is immediately confronted with the problem of how to deal with the immense secondary literature. One could easily spend a lifetime just cataloguing it. One is forced, finally, to make use of a maxim attributed to "an old chemist" by C. S. Peirce: "*Lege, lege, lege, labora, ora, et relege.*"[1] Beyond that, what is one to do? The convention of relegating to the notes the relevant secondary literature has been chosen in the hopes of avoiding cumbersome logomachies which would make the narrative read more awkwardly than it already does. Rather than have Kant's numerous critics speak for him, let him speak for himself. This is appropriate for several reasons.

First, one must often be concerned with writings which have not really been given thorough treatments by Kant's commentators. Secondly, most of the literature is either too technical to serve the present purposes, or too specialized. Consequently, the style of presentation here is narrative rather than analytical, empathetic rather than critical. I have been less concerned with the logical precision and

---

[1] C. S. Peirce, "The Fixation of Belief," as quoted in *The Enduring Questions*, edited by Melvin Rader, third edition (New York: Holt, Rinehart and Winston, 1976), p. 193. Rader translates the maxim: "Read, read, read, work, pray, and read again."

coherence of specific pieces of argumentation than with the aspects of Kant's texts which present a broad view of his moral philosophy. Thirdly, very few secondary pieces have been found which focus directly enough on the matters which here are of concern. Those pieces which are of relevance have been represented adequately enough in the notes. And, finally, this study is sufficiently novel to make Kant's primary texts the obvious materials to use, and, therefore, the most obvious ones to cite. Furthermore, a lengthy, but still selective, bibliography of secondary sources is supplied at the end of this study.

There are two works, however, which have informed much of what is presented here. The first is Iris Murdoch's *The Sovereignty of Good*,[2] and the second, Stuart Hampshire's *Two Theories of Morality*.[3] Iris Murdoch convincingly suggests the possibility of discussing what happens "in between" specific moral choices, though she fails, remarkably, to see that what she is arguing in her book, with but a few minor alterations, is precisely what Kant had in mind. (She states throughout her book that her view is opposed to the Kantian one.) Stuart Hampshire's work confirms much of that with which the present study has been concerned to argue. His thesis, roughly, is that there are but two kinds of moral theory. One requires of its practitioners a revolution in attitudes and a thorough overturning of many settled moral beliefs. Hampshire identifies Spinoza as a theorist of this type. The other insists that moral life develops gradually as the refinement of what were before crude and parochial attitudes and beliefs. The wholesale abandonment of moral beliefs is not thought to be necessary. What is necessary is the development, over sometimes long stretches of one's life, of refined moral manners, and that these manners be simply more clearly articulated, but essentially the same moral practices as prior to the refinement. According to this theory, one's childhood morality needs civilizing adjustment. Hampshire identifies Aristotle as a proponent of such a theory. What he does not say, nor perhaps even see, is that Kant's moral theory embraces the

---

[2]Iris Murdoch, *The Sovereignty of Good* (New York: Schocken Books, 1971).

[3]Stuart Hampshire, *Two Theories of Morality* (London: Oxford University Press, 1977).

best of both of his two theories. Kant's moral theory requires the wholesale revolution of attitudes as well as the gradual refinement in practice of those attitudes. What Hampshire presents as the two possible theories of morality are simply the rationalist theory and the empiricist theory. Kant rejects them both in part, and adopts the critical aspects of each. He stands squarely in the middle with a theory which embraces the rigor of rationalist formalism without its excesses, and the practicality of the empiricist approach without its implicit relativism.

Nevertheless, both Murdoch and Hampshire can help one to see some of the broader issues of moral philosophy. What they both claim Kant overlooked is precisely the heart of his philosophy. Michel Despland's *Kant on History and Religion*[4] and William Galston's *Kant and the Problem of History*[5] have also been very helpful. Both of these books are large-scale studies of Kant's late essays on history and religion. Both are helpful in pointing out the organic relationship between Kant's critical doctrines and his "popular" works. I am indebted both to A. C. Genova for his wonderfully clear analyses of the third *Critique*,[6] and to Alan Donagan for his *The Theory of Morality*[7] which had confirmed much of what I had been gradually understanding of the relationship between the Judeo-Christian morality and Kant's moral philosophy. Finally, I have incurred an enormous debt to a fictional character, Theodore, Samuel Johnson's wise "hermit of Teneriffe."[8] Without Theodore's experiences with the chains of Habit I do not think I would have understood why Kant believed so strongly that morality cannot become habitual.

---

[4]Michel Despland, *Kant on History and Religion* (Montreal: McGill-Queen's University Press, 1973).

[5]William A. Galston, *Kant and the Problem of History* (Chicago: University of Chicago Press, 1975).

[6]A. C. Genova, "Kant's Complex Problem of Reflective Judgment," *The Review of Metaphysics* 23 (1969-1970): 452-80.

[7]Alan Donagan, *The Theory of Morality* (Chicago: University of Chicago Press, 1977).

[8]Samuel Johnson, "Vision of Theodore, Hermit of Teneriffe," in *The Works of Samuel Johnson*, a New Edition in Twelve Volumes (London: Luke Hanfard, 1806) 2:454-71.

Chapter One

The Moral Law
and
Moral Consciousness

An essay on Kant's moral philosophy should begin with a discussion of the *Groundwork of the Metaphysics of Morals,*[1] both because it is in this work that Kant introduces and argues for the categorical imperative, and because it is the work with which most students of Kant are familiar. It will be shown in what follows that in the *Groundwork* Kant intends to characterize, in passing, some of the subjective features of moral consciousness.[2]

---

[1] *Grundlegung zur Metaphysic der Sitten* (1785), 4; *Foundations of the Metaphysics of Morals,* trans. by L. W. Beck (New York: Bobbs-Merrill, 1959). Hereafter cited as *Grundlegung* and/or *Groundwork*. For the form used to cite individual volumes of *Kants Werke*, see above "Note on Kant's German Texts and Translations.")

[2] Later in the chapter the view is developed that morality consists primarily of a special kind of consciousness differing significantly from what

A reconsideration of the *Groundwork* emphasizes especially certain aspects of the effort to discover the moral law and to maintain a clear grasp of it. The method employed here is to draw heavily on passages not normally emphasized by Kant's many commentators, particularly those passages in which there are discussions of the tendencies of certain experiences to undermine moral consciousness, the subjective consequences of the loss of moral consciousness, and those passages indicating that the subjective consistency of moral life depends upon the recapture of a kind of innocence that is presented in some of Kant's later works as a revolution in the ground of a man's maxims, referred to also in the later works as the birth of new man.[3]

The concern here is to extrapolate from this major text a skeletal view of the moral life seen from the perspective of one who attempts to live it in the manner foreseen and prescribed by Kant, the problems encountered (or endured) in the attempt to live it, and the philosophical implications this view of moral life has for the efforts of students of Kant to understand the position the *Groundwork* occupies in Kant's complete moral philosophy.[4]

---

might be called "natural consciousness." The point is that morality, in Kant's sense, is a matter of what we ordinarily call "attitudes." Some attitudes (indeed, most attitudes) are non-moral. The differences between them and the moral ones can be made clear by describing each phenomenologically. I take it that Kurt Baier's "moral point of view" represents a moral attitude of sorts as well as what I am here calling "moral consciousness.".

[3] *Die Religion innerhalb der Grenzen der blossen Vernunft* (1793), 6, pp. 187ff; *Religion within the Limits of Reason Alone*, trans. by T. M. Greene and H. H. Hudson (New York: Harper and Row, 1960) pp. 43ff. Hereafter cited as *Religion*.

[4] That the *Groundwork* is not the final articulation of Kant's moral philosophy is evident. In the preface (*Grundlegung*, 4:248; Beck, p. 8) Kant has this to say: "*Gegenwärtige Grundlegung ist aber nichts mehr, als die Aufsuchung und Festsetzung des obersten Prinzips der Moralität, welche allein ein in seiner Absicht ganzes und von aller anderen sittlichen Untersuchung abzusonderndes Geschäfte ausmacht.*" The *Groundwork* is "the search for and the establishment of the supreme principle of morality." This, Kant says, should be kept separate from all other moral inquiry. Furthermore, the establishment of the supreme moral principle is unlike a metaphysics of morals in that the latter is "capable of a high degree of popularity and adaptation to the common understanding."

Discussion begins with a consideration of what Kant calls the compass of common human reason.[5] The study moves then to a discussion of the fate of common human reason in the context of four very different types of lives; two in which reason functions properly, and two in which it does not. These last two lives, it is argued, result not from the failures of the faculties but from the weakening of moral vision. These lives are oriented toward goals which produce distortions attributable to acute defects in the passions.[6]

---

[5]The notion of "common human reason" is crucial throughout the *Groundwork*. It, i.e., "*die gemeine Menschenvernunft*," (cf. *Grundlegung*, 4:260; Beck, p. 20) represents the pre-philosophical way of thinking about morals. The "*Kompass der gemeinen Menschenvernunft*" is the nonarticulated principle of morality, which nevertheless "can easily be brought to a high degree of correctness and completeness in moral matters," (*Grundlegung*, 4:247; Beck, p. 7). Kant's argument moves "analytically" from common knowledge or morality to the principle contained in that knowledge, and then after the principle has been articulated he moves "synthetically" back to common knowledge where it "finds its application." (*Grundlegung*, 4:248; Beck, pp. 8-9) The argument, therefore, repeats the familiar Kantian method of moving from the experience of something back to the conditions making that experience possible. Once the conditions are articulated clearly, i.e., once the a priori structures of experience are discovered and clarified, a return to that experience produces in it a "sea change," unlike the one in Shakespeare's *Tempest*, into something *no longer* "rich and strange." The point here is that the formal articulation of the moral law makes its mystification and deliberate obfuscation more difficult when it is taken back "synthetically" to "common knowledge." The role of the moral philosopher, in Kant's view, is to clarify and fortify what every common human being knows already, yet dimly, about morality. Common human reason is, after all, still reason—a reason innocent of the strength of its competition, unaware of its own powers.

[6]Cf. Kant's interesting discussions of the passions in *Anthropologie in pragmatische Hinsicht* (1800), 8; *Anthropology from a Pragmatic Point of View*, trans. by Mary J. Gregor (The Hague: Martinus Nijhoff, 1974). Hereafter cited as *Anthropologie*. See especially: *Anthropologie*, 8:156-67; Gregor, pp. 132-42. In paragraph 80: "*Passion (passio animi)* is an inclination that prevents reason from comparing it with the totality of all our inclinations when we are making a choice." In paragraph 81: "for pure practical reason, the passions are cancerous sores; they are, for the most part, incurable because the patient does not want to be cured and shuns the rule of principles, which is the only thing that could heal him."

The sketches of these lives confirm most of the practical and ethical wisdom of Kant's own day.[7] There is evidence that these sketches are influenced by many popular psychological and religious perspectives of Kant's own time. Writers such as David Hume, Samuel Johnson, Bernard Fontenelle, Jean-Jacques Rousseau, and Martin Luther appear to have had important influences on Kant's own descriptions of the lives of the morally lost, the misdirected and the unregenerate.[8] The influence of David Hume especially is explored.

Finally, the relationship between Kant's notion of respect for law and the notion of criticism as they appear in the *Groundwork* is examined. Respect for law, it is argued, is a disposition resulting from the constant clarification and simplification of the field of moral consciousness.[9] Respect is Kant's term for a peculiar type of subjective consistency which alone can insure moral progress in a life devoted to moral ends, because it is the sole moral incentive.[10] It is suggested here

---

[7]Much of the ethical wisdom I mention here is found in *Anthropologie* where there are presented many rich and illuminating descriptions of character types, their virtues and vices, etc. *Anthropologie* is, perhaps, Kant's most entertaining serious work because of its "anecdotal" style of presentation. Anthropology is, as Kant puts it, the study of what men have made of themselves as opposed to what nature has made of them and what they should have made of themselves.

[8]I mention Fontenelle because of Kant's reference to him in the *Critique of Practical Reason*; Rousseau because of his early influences on Kant's moral philosophy discussed in some depth in Paul Schilpp's *Kant's Pre-Critical Ethics* (Evanston, Illinois: Northwestern University Press, 1938, 1960). See especially chapter two of Schilpp's work. I mention Luther because of his widespread influence upon German thought generally and because of his descriptions of sinful dispositions. See his *Treatise on Christian Liberty*. The influence of Hume is well established. More about this influence will appear later in the chapter. Cf. Samuel Johnson's *The Idler*. See note 106 below.

[9]Once the moral law has been articulated its directives can be more easily differentiated from the directives of the inclinations. The separation of the a priori principles from the empirical inclinations is, in effect, the clarification and simplification of moral consciousness. The efforts to maintain such clarity and simplicity are dealt with thoroughly in chapter two of this essay.

[10]Though it is the sole moral incentive, i.e., the only one produced by the moral law, other incentives (also rational) supplement it. This is the topic of

that respect is directly related to the notions of conscientiousness and sincerity found in Kant's later moral writings,[11] and that the moral life depends ultimately upon candor and truthfulness rather than upon the piecemeal attempts to check each of one's own maxims against a clear and evident moral rule. The significance of my reinterpretation of the *Groundwork* will become clearer in the final two chapters of this essay.[12]

The Compass of Common Human Reason

The substantive issue addressed in the first section of the *Groundwork* concerns the integrity of the moral principle found in what Kant calls common human reason. The argument of this section moves from the identification of the moral law in the context of

---

parts of chapters two and three of this essay. In actual moral practice supplementary rational incentives prevent the collapse of moral attitudes. Morality has, thus, both aesthetic and religious dimensions without which, Kant argues, the well-intentioned moral person is circumscribed in this endeavor to maintain his purely moral posture. This point is nowhere made clearer than at the end of the third *Critique*. Cf. *Kritik der Urteilskraft* (1793), 5:533; *Critique of Judgment*, trans. by J. C. Meredith (Oxford: Clarendon Press, 1952), pp. 120-21. Hereafter cited as *K3*. Kant's argument here is that a person like Spinoza, righteous, but persuaded that there is no God, may continue on in his honest and peaceful ways, but his endeavor will be circumscribed because he cannot draw strength from the hope of an ultimate harmony of the moral and the natural worlds. The assumption of a *Moral Author* of the world makes it possible for the moral person to regulate his own notions in the light of a postulate pointing to the harmony of the disparate worlds. This matter is treated more carefully in chapters three and five of this essay.

[11]These two notions appear in *Religion*, 6:336-41; Greene, pp. 173-78, and in *Über das Misslingen aller philosophischen Versuche in der Theodicee* (1791), 6:134-38; *The Failure of All Attempted Philosophical Theodicies*, trans. by Michel Despland in his *Kant on History and Religion* (Montreal: McGill-Queens, 1973). Hereafter cited as *Theodicee*.

[12]I attempt to view the *Groundwork* in its proper setting in Kant's moral philosophy. I show later the importance of such things as character, dispositions, and attitudes in the practice of morality, thus connecting Kant's formal theory with his notions of moral practice. It is easy then to see that these things constitute the setting of the *Groundwork*.

ordinary life toward the conclusion that the continued efficacy of this law requires that a person "take a step into philosophy."[13] The necessity for a critical examination of common human reason becomes apparent, according to Kant, once it is realized that the principle it contains gets lost in a competition with the natural inclinations; a competition Kant calls a "natural dialectic."[14]

The problem is that the unreflective person, living in a "glorious innocence,"[15] has, without philosophy, no weapons with which to combat the influences of the inclinations which, when left unchecked, corrupt the moral law at its foundations. According to Kant, the efficacy of the moral law depends upon the clarity and the purity with which it is grasped. Without philosophical criticism, the original power of the moral law is weakened by sensuous motives and inclinations which confuse the uncritical person.[16] Such a person is unable to act consistently because of the conflicting incentives at the ground of his conduct.

It is Kant's view that even the most ordinary person knows the difference between right and wrong, between good and evil, if the two are presented in examples where they are clearly in competition. This is the reason Kant repeatedly insists upon the presentation of moral actions as the actions of persons who have had to make considerable sacrifices to do their duties.[17] It is in such actions that the different kinds of incentives—moral and non-moral—can clearly be distinguished. "I do not, therefore, need any penetrating acuteness in order to discern what I have to do in order that my volition may be morally good."[18]

This doctrine forms a thread running throughout most of Kant's moral writings. It is presented clearly in many places, but nowhere

---

[13]*Grundlegung*, 4:263; Beck, p. 22.

[14]*Grundlegung*, 4:263; Beck, p. 21.

[15]Ibid.

[16]Cf. note 5 above for a discussion of common human reason.

[17]Cf. examples 1 and 4 in the second section of *Grundlegung,* 4:279-80, 281; Beck, pp. 39-40, 41.

[18]*Grundlegung*, 4:260: Beck, p. 19

quite so clearly as in his essay of 1793 entitled *On the Old Saw: That May be Right in Theory but it Won't Work in Practice*, where he writes:

> In view of even the most common human reason, the concept of duty is far stronger, more *penetrating*, and more promising than any motives borrowed from the self-interested principle of happiness—provided only if it is presented to our will in detachment from, or even in opposition to, those considerations of happiness.[19]

In fact, in the *Critique of Practical Reason*,[20] Kant claims that this incentive "occurs proportionately to the purity of the law."[21] His point in these passages is that the success of the moral enterprise depends primarily upon the extent to which the moral law is not confused with principles originating in the inclinations.

It is Kant's view that, even though the concept of duty is stronger and more penetrating than other motives, there is a natural tendency in mankind to argue against its "stern edicts." This tendency is difficult to correct, for as he writes in a slightly different context, "the way of natural necessity [is] more well beaten and usable than that of freedom: but in its practical purpose the footpath of freedom is the only one on which it is possible to make use of reason in our conduct."[22] We argue against the stern edicts of duty because it is easier to follow our inclinations than it is to do our duties. This is clear especially if we think of the inclinations—the way of natural necessity—as an incline. We *lean*, following them down a slope. It is more difficult to resist them than to yield to their power. So, though

---

[19]*Über den Gemeinspruch: Das mag in der Theorie richtig sein, taugt aber nicht für die Praxis*, 6:369; *On the Old Saw: That may be Right in Theory but it Won't Work in Practice*, trans. by E. B. Ashton (Philadelphia: University of Pennsylvania Press, 1973), p. 53. Hereafter cited as *Theorie und Praxis*.

[20]*Kritik der praktischer Vernunft* (1788), 5; *Critique of Practical Reason*, trans. by L. W. Beck (New York: Bobbs-Merrill, 1956). Hereafter cited as *KPR*.

[21]*KPR*, 5:87; Beck, p. 81.

[22]*Grundlegung*, 4:315; Beck, p. 75.

the moral law is strong and penetrating, the inclinations are more alluring. To pursue the one requires struggle; to follow the other requires only abandonment to our desires.[23]

This is the setting of the *Groundwork*. There are two powers competing for attention. In the first section Kant examines how the two appear in ordinary life; in the lives, that is, of ordinary people. The inclinations appear here as powerful counterpoises to our duties. The moral law appears as the compass of common human reason. It does not appear, though, as the categorical imperative.[24]

> To be sure, common human reason does not think of it abstractly in such a universal form, but it always has it in view and uses it as a standard of its judgments.[25]

How does it appear if not abstractly? We know from our own experience that the ordinary person has never heard of the categorical imperative, but may have heard of the golden rule. Yet it is unlikely that the ordinary person brings it up as a standard of judgment.[26] So, how does one distinguish between right and wrong? In what sense can one have a law in view which is not abstractly articulated?[27]

---

[23]Cf. Section 4 of this chapter for a discussion of Hume and the notion of "yielding to the currents of nature."

[24]The categorical imperative is the articulated version of the compass of common human reason.

[25]*Grundlegung*, 4:260; Beck, p. 20.

[26]*Grundlegung*, 4:260; Beck, p. 19, Kant writes: "Inexperienced in the course of the world, incapable of being prepared for all its contingencies, I ask myself only: can I will that my maxim become a universal law? If not, it must be rejected, not because of any disadvantage accruing to myself or even to others, but because it cannot enter as a principle into a possible universal legislation, and reason extorts from me an immediate respect for such legislation." The question, in German, reads: "*Kannst du auch wollen, dass deine Maxime ein allgemeines Gesetz werde?*" Whether this last is anywhere close to the English "what if everybody did that?," at least in colloquial usage, I do not know. The point is this: already in this example the moral law appears in a form more abstract than one would expect from current "common human" beings. It is more likely that the demands of the moral law are not articulated so suddenly or so clearly.

[27]H. L. Mencken once observed that moral reasoning in concrete contexts usually assumes the following form: "First I saw opportunity, then I saw

Kant's answer seems to be that one is directly aware of it in concrete circumstances similar to those presented in the examples in the first section. There is some power in a person—a conscience, so to speak—which resists one's natural inclinations to cheat customers, to be dishonest in one's dealings with others, etc. This power, according to Kant, appears even in the life of the most malicious criminal. Here it appears as the wish to be virtuous and to do what is right. The criminal, according to Kant, despises himself for not being able to live in accordance with principles made manifest to him in the lives of the honest and steadfast people he encounters. The recognition of virtue in others seems to be one of the primary non-formal experiences of the moral law, not only for criminals but for us all before we become more practiced in the use of reason.

A particularly clear example of the presence of the moral law in experience is discussed by Kant in the *Critique of Practical Reason* where he writes:

> To a humble plain man, in whom I perceive righteousness in a higher degree than I am conscious of in my self, *my mind bows* whether I choose or not, however high I carry my head that he may not forget my superior position. Why? His example holds a law before me which strikes down my self-conceit when I compare my own conduct with it: that it is a law which can be obeyed, and consequently is one that can actually be put into practice, is proved to my eyes by the act.[28]

The imperfections of the humble plain person are, according to Kant, "not so well known to me as are my own."[29] In a footnote in the *Groundwork* in which Kant is responding to a question by Johann

---

difficulty. Next I saw danger, and finally, I saw *wrong*." One's seeing wrong, in this case, is still far removed from one's seeing that one's maxim could not be universalized. It is closer to one's seeing that one would be caught. Whether the dim appreciation of being caught is an inarticulate appearance of the moral law, or whether it is instead the bright appreciation of an immediate social context—whether, in fact, the two may be the same thing looked at from each of two different standpoints—is unclear from Kant's texts.

[28]*KPR*, 5:85; Beck, pp. 79-80.

[29]*KPR*, 5:85; Beck, p. 80.

Georg Selzer[30] concerning why theories of virtue accomplish so little even though they are convincing to reason, Kant argues that, if examples used in moral training are carefully selected to show honest and steadfast persons doing their duties in spite of great temptations to do otherwise, "even moderately young children" are impressed.[31]

It is interesting to note that in Kant's discussions of ordinary moral consciousness, the moral law appears in a way analogous to an object of sight. The "subjective restrictions and hindrances . . . far from concealing it and making it unrecognizable . . . rather bring it out by contrast and make it shine forth all the brighter."[32] The visual metaphors serve to point out the immediacy with which the moral law is grasped in ordinary life. There is a directness about its appearance.

The appearances of the moral law in non-formal settings, that is, in the ordinary experiences of people, serve as the basis upon which Kant erects his formal analysis of the categorical imperative. Its ordinary appearance can now be grasped:

1. It appears non-formally to ordinary people (not abstractly as a formalized rule).

2. Its effects are to check sensuous inclinations.

3. It is made manifest primarily in the contrast between the conduct we observe in others and what we know about ourselves.

4. It humbles our pride and makes us wish we could be more virtuous.

5. Its effects are strong and penetrating.

6. It appears normally as a power inducing us to resist various temptations to transgress our known duties.

7. It affects us especially when we are in default of ourselves.

8. It is likened to a voice of conscience similar to Socrates' *daemon*.

---

[30]Johann Georg Sulzer (1720-1770), an important figure at the court and in literary circles in Berlin.

[31]*Grundlegung*, 4:268; Beck, p. 27.

[32]*Grundlegung*, 4:253; Beck, p. 13.

9. It is *perceived* as something brilliant, shining and clear.[33]

Kant's argument in the first section of the *Groundwork* begins, thus, with an examination of ordinary moral consciousness. His effort is to isolate and describe those experiences in which the compass of common human reason appears non-formally. His procedure, here as in the *Critique of Pure Reason*,[34] is to locate the a priori conditions of morality in the experiences to which it gives rise. During the course of his examination of ordinary moral consciousness he introduces a series of discussions indicating the weakness of this ordinary consciousness and the necessity for criticizing it so that its principle is not lost. It seems that without "the step into philosophy," powerful forces in people corrupt the purity of the moral law in its foundation, thus rendering it ineffectual in life.[35]

Reflective and Non-Reflective, Moral and Amoral Lives

If common human reason and its "compass" appear so sharply in ordinary life, what is the necessity for examining it by taking a step into philosophy? Kant's answer to this question is puzzling and points to an aspect of this moral philosophy seldom dealt with by his commentators. It appears that the step into philosophy is necessitated by some kind of confusion arising in ordinary moral consciousness. To describe this confusion is one of the purposes of the final part of the first section and most of the second section of the *Groundwork*.[36]

It appears that there are basically four kinds of lives dealt with in

---

[33]This notion of perceiving the moral law as "brilliant, shining and clean" is metaphorical, to be sure. The metaphor of vision works well, though, to emphasize the directive power of a "beacon" or a "compass," terms Kant himself uses in several places. Cf. *Grundlegung*, 4:247; Beck, p. 7.

[34]*Kritik der reinen Vernunft* (1781). Hereafter cited as *K1*, with the standard A and B edition paginations. My English quotations from *K1* are from the N. K. Smith translation, *Critique of Pure Reason* (London: Macmillan, 1973).

[35]These forces are the inclinations and the passions. For a discussion of both and the differences between them see *Anthropologie*, 8:156-57; Gregor, pp. 132-33.

[36]*Grundlegung*, 4:261-65; Beck, pp. 21-25.

the *Groundwork*.[37] There are two kinds of moral lives and two kinds of amoral ones.

The moral life can be lived in two different ways, either innocently or self-consciously. There is the plain humble person, of whom Kant so often writes, whose virtue appears as a mysterious gift, a person living in the image of righteousness without the interior turmoil that usually attends the attempts at such a life.[38] The humble plain person is at peace with himself and his duties. There is a graciousness about him that is enviable. Kant argues that though grace and duty are contradictory, *the graces* attend virtue and give it a "courageous and hence joyous" temperament. Its absence is detected in the life of the person who grudgingly does his duty, which indicates, Kant says, a "slavish frame of mind." "And a heart," Kant writes, "which is happy in the *performance* of its duty (not merely complacent in the *recognition* thereof) is a mark of genuineness in the virtuous disposition—of genuineness even in *piety*, which does not consist in the self-inflicted torment of a repentant sinner."[39] The joyous, that is the *gracious*, frame of mind is an indication, Kant argues, that a person has "attained *a love* for the good," which is the incorporation of it into his maxim.

---

[37]*Grundlegung*, 4:251-52; Beck, pp. 11-12, for the person with a "cultivated reason" and "the common run of men who are better guided by mere natural instinct and who do not permit their reason much influence on' their conduct"; p. 258; Beck, p. 17, for the person who acts according to a conception of law; pp. 293-94; Beck, p. 53, where Kant writes "but fidelity in promises and benevolence in principle (not on instinct) have intrinsic worth." The person, thus, who is instinctively benevolent is not on that count judged to be morally worthy.

[38]Another way to get at the contrast I am here suggesting is to notice the two different conceptions of love in the *Grundlegung*: (1) pathological love, and (2) practical love. The first is "instinctive," the second is commanded. Kant notes that it would be contradictory to command love of the pathological kind, but not practical love. One supposes that the love of "the Holy One of the Gospel" is of the former, not the latter, kind, yet Kant argues that the commandment "Love your neighbor" would make no sense unless it were supposed to be "practical." *Eros*, apparently, is "pathological" and *agape* is "practical."

[39]*Religion*, 6:161-62n; Greene, pp. 18-19n.

Kant seems, in these passages, to waffle between two notions of the moral temperament. The picture of the man who preserves his life out of duty (compare *Groundwork*) and thus acts morally is far removed from the person with a joyous frame of mind. The first is *bitter*, the second is *gracious*, yet both do their duty. Both respect the law, yet one fears it, the other loves it. Is is possible to command that a person not just *respect* the law, but *love* it? The movement from *respect as fear* to *respect as love* represents a genuine "sea change."

In contrast with him there is the person whose innocence has been lost and who attempts to regain it self-consciously. He lives a life in strict obedience to the moral law, but the joy seems to have disappeared in his efforts to do his duties. He has lost all taste for life, but goes on living out of duty. For him, the struggle to live gives him not joy but a sense of dignity and self-respect.[40] It is important to note here that the morality of this person depends upon a sort of formal reflection apparently missing from the moral consciousness of the innocent person who is plain and humble.[41]

In addition to the morally innocent and the morally self-conscious there are two other types of persons whose lives are analogous to them. There is the naively bad person and the self-consciously bad person.[42] The naively bad person represents, for Kant, the fate of most ordinary people who out of moral weakness abandon themselves to the inclinations. They represent persons with no strength of character, persons who are undisciplined and uneducated.[43] They are buffeted

---

[40]This, of course, is the *Groundwork* picture of the moral person. See note 39 above.

[41]For an analysis of the corruption of ordinary consciousness see Martin Buber, *Good and Evil: Two Interpretations*, trans. by Ronald Gregor Smith (New York: Charles Scribner's Sons, 1953), pp. 125-43.

[42]*Grundlegung*, 4:250; Beck, p. 10: "the coolness of a villain makes him not only far more dangerous but also more directly abominable in our eyes."

[43]Cf. *Anthropologie*, 8:178; Gregor, p. 152, where Kant writes: "for a good heart is an impulse to the practical good, even if it is not exercised according to principles—so that both the good-natured man and the good-hearted man are people whom a crafty fellow can use as he pleases." Kant's point is that people with weakness of character—those on whom principles have little effect—are likely to fall into evil by following their inclinations unself-consciously. This is especially true, Kant says, of the man with a choleric temperament; p. 181; Gregor, p. 154.

about by the winds of fashion and are unable to resist the more alluring temptations.[44]

In contrast to them, the self-consciously bad person is the one who misuses reason by elevating to the level of principles his own desires. He appears in the figure of the connoisseur who has learned to rationalize his desires and consequently to routinize his life in efforts to find happiness. He appears primarily as the counterpart of the self-consciously moral person and represents especially the fate of the sophisticate unguided by the moral law.[45]

Kant presents his readers with two models of moral life and their pathological counterparts. Each of these people appears in the *Groundwork*, each of them represents for Kant total life-courses whose directions depend upon the degree to which the moral law appears in them.[46]

The innocent and the sophisticate present an interesting problem for interpreters of Kant's moral philosophy. The problem is that of deciding whether they serve only as examples of moral and immoral people with differing degrees of self-consciousness, or whether they bring into focus genuine doubts Kant had about the possibilities of living morally, or about the value of the moral life. The plain humble person who so often appears in Kant's writings is the object both of criticism and admiration. He is good-hearted, but his good deeds seem somehow to be less than genuine because they seem not to be done from principles.[47] The plain humble person is admired, his sacrifices are respected, but his life is not so deserving of merit as is the life of the person who achieves the same from principles. Similarly, the person who is naturally bad or weak is less to be feared than the person who is self-consciously so. He is not genuinely evil as his counterpart is not genuinely good.[48]

---

[44]Ibid.

[45]*Grundlegung*, 4:251-52; Beck, p. 11.

[46]See *Religion*, 6:186ff.; Greene, pp. 42ff., for a discussion of the "change of heart" necessary for morality.

[47]Cf. note 43 above.

[48]Genuine evil and good are both the products of a person's response to principles. It follows that a person unmoved by principles can be neither genuinely good nor evil.

Genuine evil and genuine goodness are both the creatures of self-conscious activity based on principle. Further, the man of self-consciousness lives a life more imperiled than the innocent. It is more difficult for him to become good if he is bad and much easier for him to fall into evil if he becomes confused about principles.[49] This is why Kant repeatedly insists upon the need for criticism.

The step into philosophy represents, for Kant, the efforts of the self-conscious individual to restore the good will that is so easily lost in the natural dialectic. The good will is restored by reflective efforts to rediscover and to permanently appropriate the moral law. This restoration is accomplished by criticism. When the light of the moral law dims within the turmoils of ordinary life so filled with temptations, special efforts are required to restore its brilliance. The model for this restoration, the effort required to produce it, is made clear by the contrast of the life in which these efforts are manifest to the three other lives in which it is absent or perverted.[50]

The picture of the virtuous life will be more easily drawn in negative images.[51] The description of the virtuous life depends upon the descriptions of those lives which are not virtuous; namely, the types of lives which most people live and with which people are most familiar. Kant suggests that the life of virtue may nowhere be found, for this is the kind of life a person ought to live, not the lives people do in fact live.[52]

The need for a critical examination of common human reason appears because of the ease with which innocence is led astray.[53] It is led astray because it is too close to the allurement of nature. The

---

[49]This is confirmed in Kant's discussion of the "natural dialectic" in *Grundlegung*, 4:261-62; Beck, pp. 21-22.

[50]Ibid.

[51]For an interesting discussion of this point see Iris Murdoch's, *The Sovereignty of Good* (New York: Schocken Books, 1971), pp. 52-53. "Goodness appears to be both rare and hard to picture. It is perhaps most convincingly met with in simple people—inarticulate, unselfish mothers of large families—but these cases are also the least illuminating."

[52]*Grundlegung*, 4:265; Beck, p. 24.

[53]*Grundlegung*, 4:261; Beck, p. 21.

natural person, about whom so much was written during the period immediately preceding the French Revolution, is a creature of immediate experience.[54] His conduct is apparently more a function of the traditions in which he is immersed, or the environment which is his home, than it is the result of the incentives arising in reflection. Nature appears to him as the primary source of motivations and the sphere of his most important interests.[55] Since he is unreflective, he is unable to transcend the morals of his own community.[56] Thus, according to Kant, his subjective life can be pictured especially as a turbulent one in which the various sources of motivation compete, producing endless vacillations and changes of moods. He is unreliable because he is impetuous. His interests are not self-produced—so his life course is not self-managed.[57]

The step into philosophy can be usefully depicted as a retreat from the immediate world to the interiority of consciousness, providing a reflective distance between a subject and the natural world, from the perspective of which the temptations of the natural world are held at arms' length and contemplated safely.[58] From behind our eyes we can see more clearly than we can from in front of them. From there our vision is more selective and purposeful. The difficulty, though, is that there is a different set of allurements here against which we must also be prepared to defend.[59]

The step into philosophy is a step away from the sensuous world

---

[54]I am thinking of Rousseau's noble savage.

[55]Cf. my account of David Hume in Section 4 of this chapter.

[56]Cf. chapter 1 of Alan Donagan's, *The Theory of Morality* (Chicago: University of Chicago Press, 1977).

[57]An excellent discussion of this point can be found in the first sections of *Beantwortung der Frage: Was ist Aufklärung* (1784), 4; "Enlightenment" in Beck's translation of *Grundlegung*. Hereafter cited as *Aufklärung*.

[58]Kant's concept of respect contains within it the notion of distance. In English, phrases like "respectful distance" capture pretty well the point being made here. In *Anthropologie* 8:15-16; Gregor, p. 13, Kant connects the notion of *abstractio* with moral ways of seeing. His point is that abstraction is a kind of distancing of one's self from the attractiveness of unimportant features.

[59]See "Preface" to *Grundlegung*.

and a step into the self. What is to be found there? According to Kant, the self is not a substantial thing.[60] Kant is not a Cartesian. The interiority of consciousness is filled with various dark secrets. Kant warns repeatedly about the illusions bred there and cautions us to separate them carefully from each other. The moral life depends finally upon the success with which we are able to clarify this region, to isolate the moral law from the other principles found there.[61] It is clear from his descriptions of the misologist in the first section that the effort to clarify this field is a difficult and lengthy one. From our reflective standpoint we are able to discern two different kinds of principles or maxims. One kind arises from our desires, the other from our reason. The first obey laws of self-interest and serve the self. The second obey the moral law and are consistent with it. These various principles or maxims function in two different ways. Each is a principle objectively and an incentive subjectively.[62] A closer look at each is in order.

A Priori and Empirical Incentives

The two kinds of principles are differentiated from each other in terms of their sources. There are a priori principles arising in reason, and empirical principles arising from experience. The a priori principles are the only ones which are objectively necessary.[63] The empirical principles, the various hypothetical imperatives, are contingent upon the desires of the subject to satisfy his longings for happiness. The problem, though, according to Kant, is that hypothetical imperatives involve necessity "only under a subjectively contingent condition, i.e., whether this or that man counts this or that as part of his happiness."[64] But according to Kant the concept of happiness

---

[60]For an interesting discussion of Kant's notion of self, see: S. Schwarzschild's "The Tenability of Herman Cohen's Construction of the Self," *Journal of the History of Philosophy* 13:3 (July 1975): 361-84.

[61]See *Grundlegung*, 4:258n; Beck, p. 17n.

[62]*Grundlegung*, 4:247; Beck, p. 7.

[63]*Grundlegung*, 4:251-52; Beck, pp. 11-12.

[64]*Grundlegung*, 4:274; Beck, p. 34.

is so indefinite that, although each person wishes to attain it, he can never definitely and self-consistently state what it is he really wishes and wills. The reason for this is that all elements which belong to the concept of happiness are empirical, i.e., they must be taken from experience, while for the ideas of happiness an absolute whole, a maximum of well-being is needed in my present and in every future condition. Now it is impossible even for a most clear-sighted and most capable but finite being to form here a definite concept of that which he really wills.[65]

Kant gives us examples of this predicament to show what he means when he claims happiness cannot be self-consistently willed. Each example indicates some finite view of happiness and the miseries that might attend its pursuit, illustrating again the necessity of a concept of happiness as a whole and the inability of finite beings to comprehend such a whole.

If he wills riches, how much anxiety, envy, and intrigue might he not thereby draw upon his shoulders? If he wills much knowledge and vision, perhaps it might become only an eye that much sharper to show him more dreadful the evils which are now hidden from him and which are yet unavoidable, or to burden his desires—which already sufficiently engage him—with even more needs! If he wills a long life, who guarantees that it will not be long misery? If he wills at least health, how often has not the discomfort of the body restrained him from excesses into which perfect health would have led him? In short, he is not capable, on any principle and with complete certainty, of ascertaining what would make him truly happy; omniscience would be needed for this.[66]

It is interesting to note here that Kant presents an array of popular conceptions of what would bring happiness: (1) riches, (2) knowledge and vision, (3) long life, and (4) health. The pursuit of each of these

---

[65] *Grundlegung,* 4:275; Beck, p. 35.

[66] *Grundlegung,* 4:251-52; Beck, pp. 11-12.

ends is likely to bring with it corresponding, but unexpected, evils. Thus, if one is successful at becoming wealthy, the happiness expected from riches is diminished by the envy and intrigue attending such riches, or one discovers one is still unhappy because one desires more wealth. One is burdened now with a more complex set of desires which are even more difficult to satisfy. [67] Regardless of how wise one may be there is no guarantee that one's wisdom will lead one to happiness, because wisdom is not the omniscience required for such pursuits.[68]

Kant supplies his readers with a series of sketches of men who pursue such goals. The most interesting sketch in the *Groundwork* is the sketch of the misologist in the first section.

> And, in fact, we find that the more a cultivated reason deliberately devotes itself to the enjoyment of life and happiness, the more the man falls short of true contentment. From this fact there arises in many persons, if only they are candid enough to admit it, a certain degree of misology, hatred of reason. This is particularly the case with those who are most experienced in its use. After counting all the advantages which they draw . . . from the sciences . . . they nevertheless find they have actually brought more trouble on their shoulders instead of gaining in happiness. They finally envy rather than despise the common run of men who are better guided by mere natural instinct and who do not permit their reason much influence on their conduct.[69]

Not only does the search for happiness bring trouble to those who pursue it, but it produces misology. This is the bitterness of the man whose repetitive efforts to acquire happiness, whose schemes to produce success, whose ambitions are finally all destroyed, and who finally envies the common, uninstructed, natural man. There is an innocence about the natural man that is enviable from the point of view of the one who has lost his innocence.[70] The reason for the failure, as we have seen, is the indeterminateness of happiness. Happiness,

---

[67]Grundlegung, 4:276; Beck, pp. 35-36.

[68]Ibid.

[69]*Grundlegung*, 4:261; Beck, p. 21.

[70]*Grundlegung*, 4:276; Beck, pp. 35-36.

according to Kant, is not something that can be sought.[71] The moral goal is to be *worthy of happiness*. If happiness cannot be sought, virtue, according to Kant, can be.[72]

The Pathology of Empirical Moral Viewpoints
A Sketch of Hume

Kant's efforts to describe, in passing, some of the pathologies of life, have finally the effect of getting his readers to see how difficult it is to separate the pure incentives of reason, arising from respect for the moral law, from the incentives arising in various subtle ways from the inclinations. The natural dialectic arising from the competition between these principles—the a priori and the empirical—usually results in some non-moral way of life.[73] The impression left with the reader is that the moral life, whatever it is, is difficult to achieve, because it is difficult to identify, since its outward shape may not reflect its inward dimensions. It may never have been lived, but it is nevertheless commanded of all men.[74]

The particular emphasis Kant places on the distorted forms of life points negatively towards the life Kant is recommending. Throughout the *Groundwork* Kant pictures the life of a man whose subjective currents guarantee that he will miss the moral life. This man is the empiricist.[75] He is the hater of reason, whose cultivated intellect should enable him to distinguish pure from impure moral principles, but who, from *indolence*, believes that all principles arise from experience and

---

[71]*Grundlegung*, 4:276; Beck, p. 36.

[72]Kant's point is that without the step into philosophy—without self-criticism—the freedom which is characteristic of morality is swallowed up by the fashions of the day. Man is at the mercy of alien powers; he is heteronomous. Heteronomy is, by definition, non-moral.

[73]"Our concern is with actions of which perhaps the world has never had an example, with actions whose feasibility might be seriously doubted by those who base everything on experience, and yet with actions inexorably commanded by reason." *Grundlegung*, 4:265; Beck, p. 24.

[74]See section 4 of this chapter for a description of the empiricist morality.

[75]*Grundlegung*, 4:277; Beck, p. 37.

who cannot believe in pure principles of morality.[76] It can be said that the *Groundwork* was written partly as a polemic directed against the views of the empiricist. The empiricist is simply a sophisticated natural man who has learned to argue away pure moral concepts.[77] A brief sketch of him will provide a foundation for a discussion of the role of criticism in Kant's moral philosophy.

Though it would be difficult to document, it is reasonable to assume that the empiricist against whom Kant argues in the *Groundwork* is modeled after the figure of David Hume, whose autobiographical reflections at the conclusion of Book 1 of the *Treatise of Human Nature*[78] serve, at least, to provide a concrete picture of the attitude, or bent of mind, Kant believed to be the most dangerous to the ends of pure morality.[79] It is in this section of the treatise that Hume presents himself to his readers as a misologist, upset with the strained and unproductive efforts to find his bearing in the world by using his reason. He is particularly wearied by his skeptical reflections.[80] Here he counsels his readers to do as he has decided to do: namely to forget the *artifice* of philosophizing and to return to a more natural attitude, in which one can lead a less strained and more enjoyable way of life. Since this section of his treatise is so rich and so relevant for the purpose of illuminating Kant's own arguments, it is discussed here in some detail. The intent here is to capture a concrete picture of the life of the man whose reflections are not guided by belief in the efficacy of rational principles or morality in order to illuminate, by contrast, the life of the virtuous man.[81]

---

[76]For a thorough discussion of this see chapter two, section 6, of this essay.

[77]*A Treatise of Human Nature*, edited by L. A. Selby-Bigge (London: Oxford University Press, 1958). Hereafter cited as *Treatise*.

[78]*KPR*, 5:78; Beck, p. 74. E.g., "empiricism uproots the morality of intentions."

[79]*Treatise*, pp. 263-64.

[80]Cf. note 51 above.

[81]*Treatise*, pp. 263-74.

The conclusion to Book 1 of the *Treatise* follows immediately upon Hume's familiar arguments on personal identity.[82] Here Hume abandons a more formal method of argumentation in favor of autobiographical reflections, arising from the apprehensions he feels about the results of his skepticism. "I find myself," he writes, "inclined to stop a moment in my present status and to ponder that voyage, which I have undertaken."[83] "My memory of past errors and perplexities, makes me diffident for the future. The wretched condition, weakness, and disorder of the faculties, I must employ in my inquiries, increase my apprehensions."[84]

Hume's perplexities are the result of his discovery that the faculties of the mind are powerless to provide us with the certainties we need in order to do science and philosophy and to live with some assurance. He had discovered that, though there is a natural tendency in men to inquire into "the causes of every phenomenon," which "is the aim of all our studies and reflections . . ., how must we be disappointed, when we learn, that this connecting tie, or energy lies merely in ourselves."[85] The failure of the attempt to discover the tie that binds a cause to its effect in some objective phenomenon proves that the mind's faculties are faulty. But what is worse, according to Hume, is that,

> the impossibility of amending or correcting these faculties, reduces me almost to despair, and makes me resolve to perish on the barren rock, on which I am at present, rather than venture myself upon that boundless ocean, which runs out into immensity. This sudden view of my danger strikes me with melancholy; and 'tis usual for that passion, above all others, to indulge itself; I cannot forbear feeding my despair, with all those desponding reflections, which the present subject furnishes me with in such abundance.[86]

---

[82] *Treatise*, p. 263.

[83] *Treatise*, p. 263.

[84] *Treatise*, p. 266.

[85] *Treatise*, p. 266.

[86] *Treatise*, p. 264.

The melancholy and despair Hume claims to feel are not just the result of discovering the defects of the faculties but a result also of "that forlorn solitude in which I am plac'd by my philosophy."[87] He fancies himself "some strange and uncouth monster, who not being able to mingle and unite in society, has been expell'd all human commerce, and left utterly abandon'd and disconsolate."[88]

Hume is estranged from the company of ordinary men both because he does philosophy while they do not, and because he "cannot prevail with himself to mix with such deformity."[89] He is estranged from his peers, the "metaphysicians, logicians, mathematicians, and even theologians,"[90] who express a hatred of his system because in it he had declared his "disapprobation" of theirs. Thus, he is alienated from the company of ordinary men as well as from his educated peers. Outwardly, he says, "I foresee on every side dispute, contradiction, anger, calumny and detraction."[91] When he looks outside himself either for knowledge or for the support of friends and company in his efforts to live, he finds no knowledge because of the failure of his faculties, and he finds no support among men either because he despises them or their systems of philosophy. Things get even worse, he claims:

> When I turn my eye inward, I find nothing but doubt and ignorance. All the world conspires to oppose and contradict me; tho' such is my weakness, that I feel all my opinions loosen and fall of themselves, when unsupported by the approbation of others.[92]

Hume is here expressing what might be called a crisis of belief or faith. His philosophy undermines even the most mundane certainties and separates him from his fellow men without whose support his own beliefs, few as they seem to be, fall away. If our faculties cannot give us

---

[87] *Treatise*, p. 264.

[88] *Treatise*, p. 264.

[89] *Treatise*, p. 264.

[90] *Treatise*, p. 264.

[91] *Treatise*, pp. 264-65.

[92] *Treatise*, p. 265.

knowledge, and our fellow men will have nothing to do with us or we with them, how are we to live? What has put him in this awful fix?

What has done it, he claims, is his tendency to follow to their conclusions the paths of strained and subtle philosophical reflections. Philosophizing *intensely* has destroyed his faith in the power of the mental faculties and isolated him from the company of his fellows. According to Hume, his philosophizing has made him myopic. For by following the paths of subtle reasonings he can see no other way of looking at things. The turn of mind produced by *strained* philosophical reflection makes him feel "nothing but a *strong* propensity to consider objects *strongly* in that view, under which they appear to me."[93] This kind of reflection seems to produce passions which are troublesome to him:

> The intense view of these manifold contradictions and imperfections in human reason has so wrought upon me, and heated my brain, that I am ready to reject all belief and reasoning and can look upon no opinion even as more probable or likely than another. Where am I, or what? From what causes do I derive my existence, and to what condition shall I return? Whose favor shall I court, and whose anger must I dread? . . . I am confounded by all these questions, and begin to fancy myself in the most deplorable condition imaginable, environ'd with the deepest darkness, and utterly deprived of the use of every member and faculty.[94]

It seems that there are but two things that can be done in this predicament. The first is to continue taking seriously the conclusions of "refined and elaborate" reasonings, in which case the contradictions and absurdities remain, and the failure of the faculties must be lived with. The second is to "establish it for a maxim, that no refined or elaborate reasoning is ever to be received,"[95] in which case all philosophy and science are cut off. Of these two, Hume says he cannot decide which to choose, but he can certainly observe what is commonly done. "Which is," he writes,

[93] *Treatise*, pp. 268-69.

[94] *Treatise*, p. 265.

[95] *Treatise*, p. 268.

that this difficulty is seldom or never thought of; and even where it has once been present to the mind, is quickly forgot, and leaves but a small impression behind it.[96]

Furthermore, he urges,

Very refined reflections have little or no influence upon us; and yet we do not and cannot establish it for a rule, that they ought not to have any influence; which implies a manifest contradiction.[97]

Most men, according to Hume, seldom if ever engage in refined and elaborate reflection, which in any case leaves such a small impression it is quickly and easily forgotten. What, therefore, can he do that would restore his faith and mend his relationship with his fellows?

Hume's solution is at once simple and natural. Nature, he argues, has fortunately seen fit to dispel "this philosophical melancholy and delirium, either by relaxing this bent of mind, or by some avocation, and lively impressions of the senses, which obliterate all these chimeras."[98] There is, it seems, some power in nature which prevents lengthy philosophizing and destroys its influence upon us. This power coerces us back into the ordinary world again and makes those previous philosophical reflections appear "cold, and strain'd and ridiculous."[99] The child, who in the midst of a tantrum holds his breath, is saved from suffocation by reflexes which operate when he loses consciousness. Similarly, strained philosophical reflections cease as soon as the despair they produce causes a relaxation of that bent of mind producing them. All we have to do, according to Hume, is yield to these "currents of nature."[100] When we do this it is possible once again to enjoy the satisfaction of ordinary life. "I dine," Hume writes, "I play a game of backgammon, I converse, and am merry with my friends."[101] He is reduced finally, he says, "to this *indolent* belief in the

---

[96]*Treatise*, p. 268.

[97]*Treatise*, p. 269.

[98]*Treatise*, p. 269.

[99]*Treatise*, p. 269.

[100]*Treatise*, p. 269.

[101]*Treatise*, p. 269.

general maxims of the world," and resolves "never more to renounce the pleasures of life for the sake of reasoning and philosophy."[102] This method, Hume contends, recaptures for him not only the pleasures of life and the company of men, but it delivers him from the tortures of reflection. After all, he asks, "under what obligation do I lie of making such an abuse of time?"[103]

But does not this solution mean that he must now "mix with such deformity" as common men? This, apparently, is how they appear only from the perspective of strained philosophical reflections. Yet Hume is still suspicious of them even when he is among them conversing and making merry. Are they not foolish and naive? Well, if so, this foolishness is not self-induced. He writes:

> If I must be a fool, as all those who reason or believe anything *certainly* are, my follies shall at least be natural and agreeable. Where I strive against my inclination, I shall have a good reason for my resistance; and will no more be led a wandering into such dreary solitudes, and rough passages, as I have hitherto met with.[104]

If it is foolish to yield to the currents of nature, it is at least "natural and agreeable." One needs a good reason to swim upstream. But what happens if he should tire of his amusements in ordinary life? His answer is interesting. He will be able to return to his philosophizing in a more natural way after he has rested his mind.

> At the time, therefore, that I am tir'd with amusement and company, and have indulg'd a *reverie* in my chamber; or in a solitary walk by a river-side, I feel my mind all collected within itself, and am naturally *inclin'd* to carry my view into all those subjects, about which I have met with so many disputes in the course of my reading and conversation.[105]

This is because, according to him,

> 'tis almost impossible for the mind of man to rest, like those

---

[102] *Treatise*, p. 270.

[103] *Treatise*, p. 270.

[104] *Treatise*, p. 270.

[105] *Treatise*, p. 271.

of beasts, in that narrow circle of objects, which are the subject of daily conversation and action, (so) we ought only to prefer that which is safest and most agreeable.[106]

Hume's solution to the problem, as I have said, is quite simple and natural. All we have to do to be delivered from the tortures of reflection is to yield to nature's currents, return into the ordinary world until such time as that, too, becomes tiresome, after which we can return to refined and elaborate reflections. Each of these movements is produced by various inclinations to which we have yielded.

From this sketch of Hume's difficulties, it can easily be seen that there is a dialectical movement between two extremes: he moves from subtle reflections, carried on at some remove from the concerns of ordinary life, across a distance produced by this reflection into ordinary dealings with men. When he gets tired of ordinary life and its amusements, he returns to these reflections, resolving not to be so troubled by them again. But the return to subtle reflection produces the same torments as before, and it must once again be abandoned in favor of amusements. His philosophizing produces the same solitude and the same passions as before. The retreat from the melancholy and despair of philosophizing into the affairs of ordinary life produces indolence and merriment.[107]

Hume's travels into the ordinary world lead him to discover the certainties of the "general maxims of the world," belief in which he regards as indolent but the pleasures of which he cannot deny.[108] His belief in the untrustworthiness of these ordinary certainties is a philosophical presupposition with him, so that, when he takes them with him into philosophy for close and skeptical examination, they are undermined along with the satisfactions they provide.[109] Thus, the

---

[106]See the wonderful character sketches in Samuel Johnson's *The Idler* for brilliant descriptions, passim, of the alternating passions. A sample has been collected in B. H. Bronson's edition of Johnson's works (New York: Holt Rinehart and Winston, 1971), pp. 185-214.

[107]*Treatise*, p. 269.

[108]Ibid.

[109]See the last paragraph of Meditation 1 and the first paragraph of Meditation 2. It is remarkable that Hume's state of mind is here similar to

significance of involvement with others in the common affairs of life disappears with the distance necessary for reflection. This undermining of conviction is the result not of reflection generally but of Hume's peculiar kind of reflection: namely, reflecting on the objects of experience *intensively* or viewing them *strongly* from a skeptical standpoint, which, like Descartes',[110] is open only to principles which are absolutely certain no matter how they are viewed.

The epistemological point here is an important one; the certainties of everyday life cannot withstand the pressures of skeptical reflection, yet these same certainties, no matter how fragile they might be, are necessary for daily living. Hume seems to recognize this but is unable to accept it. For him, it is not philosophically respectable to rely on a steady faith in maxims which cannot withstand reflections of his kind. As a result, he must endure the torments of the rapidly alternating passions arising from his failed commitments. He cannot believe that there is anything worthy of a steady commitment and a rational faith short of absolute certainty which can be found neither in common life nor in skeptical reflections.[111] From the *intense* skeptical position there are no objects of faith outside himself on which he can rely, and only ignorance and confusion inside. The descent into common life is for Hume merely an escape from the tortures of reflection into a sphere in which all seems taken for granted, a sphere providing amusements which temporarily satisfy his longings for stability by blocking or

---

Descartes'. The difference, of course, is that in doubt Descartes discovers himself, while Hume claims not to have found himself even though it is he who is being tortured by reflection.

[110]Cf. *K1*, A744-46; B772-74, for a discussion of Hume, Knowledge and Faith; also, "Opining, Knowing, and Believing," A820-30; B848-58.

[111]I have pictured the misologist here not as a ridiculous figure, but as a tragic one. If one remembers Sancho in Don Quixote one is able to see the empiricist pictured as ridiculous compared to the hero. My picture of Hume is the picture of a man in despair. The movement from natural consciousness to skeptical reflectivity and the consequent despair is best captured by Hegel in the preface to *The Phenomenology of Mind*, translated by J. B. Baillie (New York: Harper and Row, 1967), p. 135. The movement is likened to travel on a road: "the road can be looked on as a path of doubt, or more properly, a highway of despair."

suspending reflection. He is unable to find any mode of living between strained reflection and its suspension.[112]

This sketch of Hume was intended primarily as a picture of a kind of life characterized by oscillating moods and the absence of commitments resulting from the conviction that worthy and permanent objects of knowledge cannot be found where they ought to be found in experience. This is the picture of a man whose longing for the certainties he once found as a child in a glorious innocence is frustrated when he can no longer find or respect them.[113] He has discovered in his newly found ability to reflect that the things which had served as the guideposts of his life before no longer work, and that when he is thrown back upon his own resources he cannot manage to produce convictions necessary for a steadfast involvement in ordinary life.

This is precisely what Kant means when he says that glorious innocence cannot maintain itself. The skeptical reflectivity which takes its place undermines its certainties. Kant sees that unguided reflectivity is more dangerous to the ends of moral life than is a naively natural attitude.[114] The certainties of ordinary life preserved in the general maxims of the world and believed by the natural man actually work from time to time even though they have not been refined or purified. These same certainties are destroyed by the reflective man whose reflections are not guided properly. The abuse of reflective capacity is worse than having none at all. This is at the basis of Kant's convictions that the man of good temperament, even though he does not act from principle, can be the object of admiration, if not of respect, while the reflective man's worth depends more clearly upon principles which are

---

[112]The notion of innocence in *Grundlegung,* 4:261; Beck, p. 21, recurs in *Religion*, 4, passim. However, Kant writes also of original predisposition to evil in that work. Indeed, there may be an innocence of the fact of original evil that characterizes youth. See John S. Dunne's, *Time and Myth* (South Bend: University of Notre Dame Press, 1973), for a brilliant discussion of these themes.

[113]*Grundlegung*, 4:250; Beck, p. 10.

[114]The theme of the recapture of innocence in Kant is a bit strained here, I believe. This tension seems to disappear once the reader realizes the popularity of the theme in the literature of Kant's day. See especially Wordsworth's *Intimations of Immortality* and *Tintern Abbey*.

likely to be undermined by his own reflection. His loss of innocence produces in him a despair, the escape from which requires something other than the attempt to return to a primal innocence in which reflection is suspended.[115]

Though we cannot recapture the innocence of childhood in reflection, it is possible, according to Kant, to recapture in a special kind of reflection some of the values that were found to be worthy of faith.[116] To do this, these values must be purified of their empirical components. Criticism is a method designed to rescue the moral law from the relentlessness of skeptical reflectivity.[117] Once the moral law is rescued it then serves as the "beacon" in the light of which a life of steadfast commitment becomes possible. A discussion of the role of criticism in Kant's moral philosophy will make it possible to begin to picture the moral life as it is seen from the perspective of one who attempts to live it as Kant foresaw and described it.

[115]Cf. KI, A779-80; B807-808, for a discussion of some of these values.

[116]Cf. KI, A758-69; B786-97, a section entitled "The Impossibility of a Skeptical Satisfaction of Pure Reason in its Internal Conflicts."

[117]Grundlegung, 4:262; Beck, p. 22: "In this case, as in the theoretical, it will find rest only in a thorough critical examination of our reason."

Chapter Two

Moral Incentives
and
Moral Self-Criticism

Kant's picture of life without moral convictions is a dreary one. Life is a turbulent sea—the categorical imperative supplies the impetus necessary to navigate through the turbulence by generating its own powerful incentives. However, this guidance and these incentives are ineffective without a proper attentiveness to the moral law. Kant had demonstrated already in the first section of the *Groundwork* that the moral law appears in ordinary life as the compass of common human reason. What he means by "compass" is quite clear. A "compass" is a direction-finder. The moral law is that compass both in ordinary life and in a more reflective philosophical posture. In ordinary life, however, the compass is obscured much of the time. It is for this reason that Kant insists that special efforts are required to destroy or diminish the forces which obfuscate the moral law.

The effort of the second section of the *Groundwork* is to discover a method by which the moral law can be lifted out of those contexts of ordinary life in which it becomes confused with other less worthy principles arising from the inclinations.[1] Reason, the source of the moral law, can become practical, according to Kant, only when it "directly determines the will."[2] What happens when it is obscured can already be seen in the preceding sketch of Hume's predicament. The incentives driving the will appear and then disappear, producing oscillations of mood and vacillations in motives. The man in this predicament is morally lost because no reliable guides are available to him. Reason cannot determine the will just to the extent that other incentives lessen its power. The way out of this difficulty, according to Kant, is to clarify and purify the field of consciousness, separating sharply those incentives arising from reason from those arising elsewhere. This process of clarification is *criticism*.[3]

Kant's view is that philosophizing is the active clarification of the field of consciousness. It is not, for him, a passive contemplation of eternal verities or of the rapidly changing contents of a confused mind. Criticism, for Kant, is an endless and difficult labor. If it succeeds in freeing the moral law from the confusions which obscure it, it does not do it once and for all time.[4] After all, the inclinations survive as long as a person lives, and they must be repeatedly consigned to their proper place and refined so that they will not destroy the values they can be made to serve. Criticism must continue throughout life, and the more practiced we become in doing it the more permanent and reliable will be its fruits. Its primary task is to lift the "compass of common human

---

[1] *KPR*, 5:79; Beck, p. 74: "What is essential in the moral worth of actions is that the moral law should directly determine the will."

[2] *Grundlegung*, 4:268-69; Beck, pp. 28-29: "It is only in this manner that pure moral dispositions can be produced and engrafted on men's minds for the purpose of the highest good in the world."

[3] *Grundlegung*, 4:269; Beck, p. 28; "it is evident that it is not only of the greatest necessity in a theoretical point of view but also of the utmost practical importance to derive the concepts of laws of morals from pure reason and to present them pure and unmixed."

[4] *KI*, A812-13; B840-41n; "It is necessary that the whole course of our life be subject to moral maxims; but it is impossible that this should happen unless reason connects with the moral law an outcome, either in this or in another life, that is in exact conformity with our supreme ends."

reason" out of the confusions which surround it in ordinary life.[5] In Kant's work, the clarified compass of common human reason appears as the categorical imperative, respect for which produces the incentives necessary both for its continued clarification as well as for the kind of life it commands we live.

Kant's conviction, at least in the *Groundwork* and in the *Critique of Practical Reason*, is that the purified moral law provides its own incentives and directly determines the will. But it cannot do its work if it is not clearly grasped. *That* it works for those who have grasped it is a fact, Kant argues, that cannot be denied. Its effect on us is the subjective feeling Kant calls "respect." What is extraordinary, according to Kant, is that reason, which produces the categorical imperative, can have an effect on feeling. Though Kant often suggests that the workings of reason on us are difficult to understand, the real surprise is that its effects can be felt.[6] Our job, therefore, is to learn to recognize its effects on us. Its most obvious effect, Kant says, is the *respect we feel for it*.[7]

Respect, Kant argues, is the effect of the "direct determination of the will by the law and the consciousness of this determination."[8] It is a feeling unlike others in that it is "self-wrought by a rational concept."[9]

> What I recognize directly as a law for myself I recognize with respect, which means merely the consciousness of the submission of my will to a law without the intervention of

---

[5]*Grundlegung,* 4:321; Beck, p. 80. Kant writes: "But since experience can exemplify the relation of cause to effect only as subsisting between two objects of experience, while here pure reason by mere Ideas (which furnish no object for experience) is to be the cause of an effect which does lie in experience, an explanation of how and why the universality of the maxim as law (and hence morality) interests us is completely impossible for us men." Also at *KPR,* 5:79-80; Beck, p. 75: "For how a law in itself can be the direct determining ground of the will (which is the essence of morality) is an insoluble problem for the human reason."

[6]See Footnote 2 in *Grundlegung,* 4:257-58; Beck, pp. 17-18.

[7]*Grundlegung,* 4:258n; Beck, p. 18.

[8]*Grundlegung,* 4:257; Beck, p. 17.

[9]Ibid.

other influences on my mind (*Gemuet*).[10]

Kant uses different terms to describe the effects of the law on us when we recognize it: he refers to it as a "feeling," as a kind of "consciousness," and as a "recognition."[11] It is important to insist upon the appropriateness of each of these terms.

Respect for law is indeed a feeling, but it is more than that. It is both sensuous and intellectual at the same time, as are most moods. In the *Critique of Practical Reason*[12] Kant says that respect is *felt* in two different ways. It is felt first as something negative. This negative feeling is the result of being "humbled" by something powerful, something which "checks the inclinations," "humbles my pride," and "strikes down self-love."[13] The second way in which it is felt is positive, for it is the feeling that arises when we recognize that we are being *guided* by something of *inestimable worth.*[14] This last and positive effect of the direct determination of the will by the moral law is a feeling, Kant says, which is akin to admiration but which is both more lasting and impossible to resist. It is more profound than admiration, a feeling Kant reserves for the things of nature which are beautiful but not sublime. There are but two things which produce respect: the moral law, and persons in whose actions its effects seem manifest. Persons, Kant says, are worthy of respect insofar as they are rational, insofar as they are ends-in-themselves, insofar as they are self-determined, and insofar as they are the members of an intelligible world.[15] But a discussion of the senses in which persons are worthy of

---

[10]Ibid.

[11]*KPR*, 5:80ff.; Beck, pp. 78ff.; Kant's discussion here is of the negative and positive effect of the law.

[12]*KPR*, 5:85; Beck, pp. 79-80.

[13]*KPR*, 5:85-86; Beck, pp. 79-80. See also *K3*, 5, *Critique of Aesthetic Judgment*, paragraph 28, pp. 332-36; Meredith, pp. 109-14.

[14]*Grundlegung*, 4:313-14; Beck, p. 73: "Thus categorical imperatives are possible because the idea of freedom makes me a member of an intelligible world."

[15]For two excellent articles on the relationship between "respect" and "persons" see A. M. MacBeath, "Kant on Moral Feeling." *Kant-Studien* 64

respect would carry us beyond the purposes of this chapter.[16]

What is to be preserved here is the point that respect for law is a feeling with both elevating and humiliating effects. Both of these effects insure, while they are felt, that the moral law is the primary object of attention in the field of consciousness.[17] Respect is a feeling resulting from the suppression of competing incentives and the awakening of rational ones. As such it can be characterized as a form of consciousness in which things of moral value appear and can be seen clearly. It is Kant's view that things of moral worth appear only in this subjective attitude.[18]

It can be said that the "moral world" appears only to the person whose consciousness is open to it.[19] The most important effect of the moral law upon us is, therefore, to allow the moral dimensions of our experience to appear clearly to us. It is only after this happens that the question of how to deal with particular difficulties can be addressed seriously.[20]

(1973): 283-314; and Milton C. Nahm, " 'Sublimity' and the 'Moral Law'," *Kant-Studien* 50 (1958/1959): 502-24. See especially MacBeath, pp. 300-304.

[16]*KPR*, 5:89; Beck, p. 83. "The feeling which arises from the consciousness of this constraint is not pathological, as are those caused by objects of the senses, but practical, i.e., possible through a prior (objective) determination of the will and the causality of reason."

[17]*Grundlegung*, 4:312-13; Beck, p. 72: "But now we see that, if we think of ourselves as free, we transport ourselves into the intelligible world as members of it and know the autonomy of the will together with its consequence, morality; while, if we think of ourselves as obligated, we consider ourselves as belonging both to the world of sense and at the same time to the intelligible world."

[18]Ibid.

[19]Awareness of the "Kingdom" precedes acting on its behalf. This is developed in chapters three and five.

[20]MacBeath's (cf. note 15 above) rather typifies the sort of interpretation of Kantian moral philosophy to which I am objecting. After having written an insightful piece on Kant's notion of moral feeling, he concludes that all of Kant's talk about moral feeling is finally "dispensable" and can be replaced with "good reason" talk. "Thus we may say: One's action is morally praiseworthy only if the reason for one's acting thus was (or perhaps, if a sufficient reason for one's acting thus would have been) a good (i.e., a moral)

reason" (p. 311). MacBeath supports his view that all the "moral feeling" talk could be replaced with "good reason" talk by citing P. R. Foot's treatment of the subject. Foot, like MacBeath, believes that "what Kant thinks to be the special, inescapable nature of morality and its demands is simply a distorted reflection of morality as it is in fact taught: we grow up *feeling* bound to do certain kinds of things, and it is confused awareness of this sort of feeling that results in talk of moral demands as being essentially categorical or unconditional" (p. 313n). MacBeath concludes his analysis thus: "Kant goes most seriously wrong: reason discourse and cause discourse are not, as he thinks, appropriate to two different, mutually exclusive kinds of human action, but offer complementary accounts of the same action. The doctrine of moral feeling has this mistake at its basis, but what is so astonishing is that a theory which attempts to prove the existence of a feeling a priori, and to guarantee freedom of the will on the basis of that feeling, that a theory so breathtakingly absurd, should prove as rewarding as it does" (p. 314). MacBeath is wrong on each count of his indictment. First, talk about moral feeling is not dispensable; secondly, reason discourse and cause discourse, for Kant, *are* "complementary accounts of the same actions" (that is the whole rationale behind the doctrine of the "two standpoints"); and, thirdly, Kant does not "guarantee freedom of the will on the basis of" moral feeling.

The problem with this kind of interpretation is that it reduces (or attempts to reduce) Kantian moral philosophy to a kind of myopic meta-ethic current in discussions of contemporary moral problems. Another well-known example of this is Frankena's treatment of Kant in his *Ethics* (Englewood Cliffs: Prentice-Hall, Inc., 1973), where "Kant's Theory" (pp. 30-33) is characterized as "a monistic kind of rule deontology" which differs from utilitarian theories at this point and that. Frankena repeats a depressing bill of standard objections to Kant's theory: (1) it doesn't account for conflict of duty; (2) it leads one to conclude that lying is always wrong; (3) it doesn't supply a foolproof criterion for deciding whether certain maxims are even in the domain of moral discourse (one can, for example, "universalize" the maxim to whistle in the dark when alone); (4) his criterion of right and wrong is insufficient; and finally, (5) "there is more to the moral point of view than being willing to universalize one's rules; Kant and his followers fail to see this fact, although they are right in thinking such a willingness is part of it" (p. 33).

The mistake made by MacBeath and Frankena is a common one. They suppose Kant and all other historical moral philosophers to be engaged in a current philosophical controversy, and that, e.g., Kantian moral philosophy should, therefore, observe the current limitations on debate, fall neatly into the current meta-ethical taxonomies, and be cooperatively respondent to a fashionable list of questions. The kind of taxonomical formalism imposed, therefore, on Kantian moral philosophy is far worse than the formalism with which Kant is charged. The limits put on discourse by the taxonomy rules out a priori nearly all of the nuances that make Kant's moral philosophy worth examining.

The failure to recognize this sequence has been the mistake of many of Kant's interpreters.[21] They have led their students, especially, to believe that Kantian morality consists exclusively of the checking of "maxims" against the categorical imperative as it is found in Kant's work.[22] This—as if to say that *acting* morally can precede *being* moral. Kantian morality is not a mechanism or a calculus, regardless of how many interpreters have taken it to be such. The problem of *moral judgment* in Kant's work occupies one part, and one part only, of his moral philosophy. He does not really begin to discuss the problem of *moral judgment* until he is satisfied that he has been clear about the conditions necessary for its possibility.[23] The problem of *moral character* in Kant has been neglected by many of his commentators because they seem to believe that that is what he is discussing in the *Groundwork*.[24] But neither can this problem be confronted here. It will be the topic of the next chapter. The point here is that moral judgment can be nothing more than a nonsensical routine when it is carried out by someone who is not already living in the light of the moral law.[25] Attempts to live this life in reverse, *to become moral by judging*, indicates a moral naiveté dealt with humorously by Kant in many of his later works, especially in the *Religion*.

---

[21]Cf. my discussion of moral judgment in chapter three below.

[22]One must already have adopted a moral outlook before the problem of judgment is even relevant. It is the problem of describing that outlook, and even its possibility, to which Kant first turns. Cf. chapters three and five below.

[23]Moral judgment is more than the checking of maxims. It includes, indeed begins with, self-examination. Cf. chapter three below. Also see Nahm's " 'Sublimity' and the 'Moral Law' " cited in note 15 above, for a discussion of "the object of moral judgment."

[24]Ibid.

[25]Cf. *Vorlesungen über Logik*, 8:341-45; *Logic*, trans. by Robert Hartmann and Wolfgang Schwarz (New York: Bobbs-Merrill, 1974), pp. 25-30. Hereafter cited as *Logic*. See especially p. 343. Hartmann, pp. 28: "The mere theoretician or, as Socrates calls him, the *philodoxus*, strives only after speculative knowledge, without caring how much his knowledge contributes to the ultimate end of human reason; he gives rules for the use of reason to all kinds of ends. The practical philosopher, the teacher of wisdom through

Kant's view is that a grasp of the moral law is a prerequisite for moral judgment, and that such judgment requires, as does criticism, much practice and great labor.[26] Much of the labor of moral practice consists of developing the ability to distinguish the feeling of respect from the countless other feelings with which we are bombarded. Though Kant describes the feeling of respect in sections of the second *Critique*, in the *Groundwork* he offers more formal accounts of it.

Thus, Kant characterizes respect in three different ways: (1) as a feeling differing from other feelings in that it is "self-wrought by a rational concept, "[27] (2) as the consciousness "of the submission of my will to a law,"[28] and (3) as "all so-called moral interest."[29] All are the subjective effects of the law on a subject attentive to the moral law. It is especially important to notice that Kant here distinguishes respect from "obscure feelings" both in terms of its source—its cause—and in terms of its phenomenological tone or, perhaps, its extent.[30] Its source is a rational concept, the moral law, and its tone is less like a feeling such as a pain or a discomfort than it is like an attitude, a disposition, or a mood. It is, as he says, a *consciousness* produced by the submission of the will to a law.[31]

This consciousness is characterized chiefly by the clarity and focus of its object as well as by its consistency and its certitude. There are

---

doctrine and example, is the philosopher in the true sense. For philosophy is the idea of a perfect wisdom that shows us the ultimate ends of human reason." I am constructing a similar analogy here. Learning how to make moral judgments without first an appreciation of the moral world to which these judgments are directed amounts to a sort of *philodoxy* whose results are, at best, a shadow of morality. As everywhere else in Kant's philosophy, the ground must be prepared before anything planted in it can be expected to bear fruit.

[26]Cf. the discussion of moral discipline in chapter three.

[27]*Grundlegung*, 4:257; Beck, p. 17.

[28]Ibid.

[29]Ibid.

[30]Cf. Nahm, " 'Sublimity' and the 'Moral Law'," and MacBeath, "Kant on Moral Feeling," for a discussion of this tone. Also see chapters three and five below.

[31]*Grundlegung*, 4:257; Beck, p. 17.

many passages in Kant's moral writings in which these characteristics are given more adequate expression. For our purpose here, which is to characterize criticism as it is performed in a moral context and to contrast it with the confused consciousness which it is designed to supplant, it is instructive to introduce one of the examples Kant gives of this process in his essay of 1793 on theory and practice.[32] The example, so important here, will be cited in full so that the contrast between clear and confused moral consciousness will be evident:

> Suppose, for instance, that someone is holding another's property in trust (a deposit) whose owner is dead, and that the owner's heirs do not know and can never hear about it. Present this case even to a child of eight or nine, and add that, through no fault of his the trustee's fortunes are at lowest ebb, that he sees a sad family around him, a wife and children disheartened by want. From all of this he would be instantly delivered by appropriating the deposit. And further that the man is kind and charitable, while those heirs are rich, loveless, extremely extravagant spendthrifts, so that this addition to their wealth might as well be thrown into the sea. And then ask whether under these circumstances it might be deemed permissible to convert the deposit to one's own use. Without a doubt anyone asked will answer "No!"—and in lieu of grounds he can merely say: "It is wrong!", i.e., it conflicts with duty. Nothing is clearer than that. And assuredly it is not his own *happiness* that the man promotes by surrendering the deposit. For if happiness were the end that he expected to determine his decision, he might, for example, think along these lines: "If you give up, unasked, what does not belong to you, you will gain a widespread good reputation that may become quite lucrative for you." But all this is very uncertain. On the other hand, many misgivings arise as well: "To end your straitened condition at one stroke, you might embezzle what has been entrusted to you; but if you made prompt use of it, you would evoke suspicions concerning how and by what

---

[32] *Theorie und Praxis*, 6. See note 19 above.

means your circumstances had so quickly improved; however, if you were slow about it, your distress would increase in the meantime to a point beyond help."

The will thus pursuant to the maxim of happiness vacillates between motivations, wondering what it should resolve upon. For it considers that outcome, and that is most uncertain: one must have a good head on his shoulders to disentangle himself from the jumble of arguments and counter-arguments and not to deceive himself in the tally. But if he asks himself where his duty lies, he is not in the least embarrassed for what answer to give himself; he is instantly certain what he must do. In fact, if the concept of duty carries any weight with him, he will actually shudder to think of the benefits he might derive from its violation, just as if he still had a choice.[33]

To readers of the *Groundwork* this passage has a familiar tone. Its argument is recognizable and easy to follow: the motive of duty (the necessity of an action done from respect for law), Kant argues, provides, in this example at least, a clarity and certainty, a simplicity and an efficacy not to be found among the motives arising from a consideration of happiness. We cannot be certain of the outcome when we act according to motives of self-love. Our minds vacillate from one possible outcome to another.[34] We find ourselves in a real stew, we are confused. Only our duty is clear and certain. The guidance we get from the moral law is straightforward and permanent, according to Kant.

The point to be stressed here is Kant's claim that the consciousness of duty exhibits a consistency and a simplicity—a penetratingness—that cannot be found among other competing motives.[35] To return to the analogy of vision, a consciousness fastened on the moral law does not lose its focus. It is not distracted and does not, therefore, vacillate between "objects." Now if we are to understand what Kant means by respect, we will have to regard it as the "feeling" of being restrained by

---

[33] *Theorie und Praxis*, 6:369-70; Ashton, pp. 53-54.

[34] Ibid.

[35] Ibid.

the moral law. The consciousness of duty is a consciousness that is singularly *directed*—it is simple in the sense of not being "duplex."[36] In the language of the *Groundwork*, the moral imperative is "categorical" and not "hypothetical."[37] The hypothetical imperatives rest upon ends which are finally indeterminable so far as those ends are bound up with happiness. Put in other words, duty is clear (at least in this particular case); it is capable of directing consciousness consistently.

This subjective consistency produced by the recognition of duty is part of what Kant calls "respect."[38] It is Kant's view that the attention of a subject is "commandeered" by that subject's recognition of his duty. What we *feel* when we are conscious of, that is, "bound by," duty is the *feeling* Kant calls "*Achtung.*"[39] This use of "respect" is not far from the ordinary use of it in contexts where we are in the presence of people who "command respect."

The moral law does its work on us if we have stepped into philosophy and criticized the principles found in ordinary moral consciousness. Once this has been done, according to Kant, the vacillations between different empirical incentives, so clearly seen in the sketch of David Hume, are dampened by the guidance of the moral law as it acts on us. It has been shown that the primary effect of the moral law on us is the production of a state of consciousness and a feeling which Kant calls respect. Respect, as can be seen, is not a mere shibboleth in Kant's moral philosophy.[40] It is his term for the consciousness open to a previously hidden moral dimension of experience, which consciousness is produced by the recognition of the moral law.[41]

N/3.

---

[36]Cf. Kant's discussion of "duplicity" in the concluding remarks of *Theodicee.*

[37]*Grundlegung*, 4:271-72; Beck, p. 31.

[38]*Grundlegung*, 4:257; Beck, p. 17.

[39]Ibid.

[40]See especially Nahm, " 'Sublimity' and the 'Moral Law'."

[41]Cf. *K1*, A808; B836: "I entitle the world a *moral world*, insofar as it may be in accordance with all moral laws; and this is what by means of the freedom of the rational beings it *can be*, and what according to the necessary laws of morality it *ought to be.*"

This consciousness is a simplified one. The moral man is steadfast in his duties not because he has found the "mechanism of morality" which would enable him to "check" his maxims, but because he is inwardly conscientious and unconfused.[42] Once he has felt the power of this law, he realizes that he is capable of living morally. And even though his previous sensuous interests have taken the back seat to moral ones, he looks forward to a continual improvement in his life with a sense of dignity.[43] This process of improvement Kant calls "reformation."[44] It occurs after what he calls "a revolution in a man's way of thinking."[45] Kant's terms appear in his later works, especially in the *Religion*[46] and in the *Anthropology*.[47] I introduce them here in order to emphasize the biographical direction of the life of the moral man.[48] In his life, sometime or other, a revolution occurs in his way of thinking. He is now able to see clearly the moral dimensions of experience. After this revolution comes what Kant calls "reformation," which can be described as the struggle for moral improvement.[49] Reformation, according to Kant, is primarily a struggle of two kinds: (1) a struggle to maintain clear moral vision through criticism, and (2) a struggle to live in the light of this vision.[50] This last struggle requires what Kant calls moral judgment. Moral

---

[42]Cf. Concluding remarks of *Theodicee.*

[43]*K1,* A819; B847.

[44]*Religion,* 6:184ff.; Greene, pp. 40ff.

[45]Ibid.

[46]Ibid.

[47]*Anthropologie,* 8:187; Gregor, p. 159: "gleich einer Art der Wiedergeburt," etc.

[48]Ibid.

[49]Cf. the notion of reformation in *Religion,* 6:187; Greene, p. 43: "*this* cannot be brought about through the gradual *reformation* so long as the basis of the maxims remains impure, but must be effected through a *revolution* in a man's disposition. . . . He can become a new man only by a kind of rebirth, as it were a new creation (John 3:5; compare also Genesis 1:2), and a change of heart.

[50]Cf. the discussion of moral discipline in chapter three below.

judgment is not the use of a set of rules for the application of the   *N B*
categorical imperative.[51]

Moral judgment, as I have indicated, is the effort of the man whose way of thinking has been transformed, who has undergone a "change of heart" and who has been "reborn" to live now in a world which is not particularly receptive to such efforts.[52] The direction of this life course is what Kant calls *vocation*.[53] A vocation can be here defined as the continuing expression of the uniqueness of a self living in the light of the moral law.[54] This struggle, according to Kant, is less the application to concrete cases of a moral rule than it is the use of a natural talent continually sharpened in a practice which can never be totally perfect.[55] There are no short cuts to moral living, according to Kant. There are, unfortunately, no rules for the application of rules.[56] Judgment is required to live in the light of the moral law. This activity of judging is the focus of the next chapter in which the "practical" aspects of Kant's moral theory will be discussed.[57] There, discussions focusing upon passages in many of Kant's later and less well-known works will be developed in order to clarify this important dimension of the moral life Kant is recommending to us.

---

[51]Cf. the discussion of judgment in chapter three below.

[52]*Religion*, 6, passim; Greene, passim.

[53]See *K1*, A819; B847, for a discussion of vocations.

[54]Cf. Nahm, " 'Sublimity' and the 'Moral Law',"

[55]See the discussion of this in chapters three and four.

[56]See the discussion of judgment in chapter three.

[57]This is discussed also in chapter five.

Chapter Three

The Doctrine of Judgment
and
Moral Discipline

The purpose in the previous chapters was to emphasize primarily the subjective effects of the moral law on the life of a person conscious of it. It was argued that this consciousness attenuates the oscillations of mood and attitude that result from the absence of the clear apprehension of moral principles. It was shown that the attempt to live in accordance with the "currents of nature" produces a skepticism resulting in a withdrawal, in Hume's case, from ordinary life in a community to distanced and strained philosophical reflections. The mundane convictions required for the enjoyment of that life were undermined. But since the strains of philosophical reflection failed to recover even the most basic of truths, leaving the skeptic in dreary despair, he was compelled to relax the philosophic bent of mind for the descent again into a deformed community imperfectly ordered by "common maxims of the world." The skeptical philosopher's stay there lasted only as long as it was necessary for him to recover the strength and the desire necessary to return again to strained reflections. The life of this man was shown to be a stormy one.

It was Kant's contention, it was argued, that for such a person the only cure was to take the step into a different kind of philosophy, one whose methods made possible the clarification and simplification of consciousness, thus making possible the reappropriation of a priori moral principles which had previously been lost. It was Kant's view, it was argued, that the task of moral philosophy to begin with was to separate the a priori moral principles from principles originating in the inclinations. Once this task was accomplished the a priori moral principles would themselves generate the incentives efficacious enough to induce a stability in what had previously been a stormy life. Remarks were focused on a discussion of Kant's notion of common human reason, the moral law embodied in it, and the subjective attitude engendered by its recognition. This attitude Kant calls "respect." The effects of this attitude on the life of one possessing it were then described. In this chapter a more thorough account of these effects will be developed.

Introduction

Here an account of Kant's doctrine of judgment will be presented in an attempt to show how it is intimately connected with a much-neglected aspect of Kant's critical philosophy which is fully developed toward the end of *The Critique of Pure Reason*. It will be argued that "The Discipline of Pure Reason"[1] contains a notion of discipline clearly enough articulated to serve as the clue, if not the key, to the solutions to problems arising from attempts to connect Kant's moral theory to moral practice. The formal apparatus of Kant's moral philosophy, its theory, has received nearly exhaustive treatment in the literatures dealing with Kant's work. The connection of this theory to practice has, however, been mistakenly assumed to be found exclusively in Kant's discussions of the universality of maxims and in his discussions of the content of the categorical imperative. It will be argued that no matter how clearly one is able to represent to oneself the

---

[1] *K1*, A709-94; B737-822.

formal doctrine of Kantian moral theory, even down to the minutest details of its perfect and imperfect duties, one is still left with what must be the profoundest of problems. This problem is the problem of *obedience.*

Moral theory clearly enough articulated does, according to Kant, guide and encourage correct moral practice, but it does not and cannot insure it. The study of moral theory is not enough according to Kant. Near the end of *The Critique of Practical Reason* Kant addresses the issue of using the faculty of judgment for the observation of the "great design" of a priori moral principles:

> But this occupation of the faculty of judgment, which makes us feel our own powers of knowledge, is not yet interest in actions and their morality itself. It only enables one to entertain himself with such judging and gives virtue or a turn of mind based on moral laws a form of beauty which is admired but not yet sought ("Honesty is praised and starves"). It is the same with everything whose contemplation produces subjectively a consciousness of the harmony of our powers of representation by which we feel our entire cognitive faculty (understanding and imagination) strengthened; it produces a satisfaction that can be communicated to others; but the existence of its object remains indifferent to us, as it is seen only as the occasion for our becoming aware of the store of talents which are elevated above the mere animal level.[2]

The remarkable thing about philosophers is that, though they admire mighty intellectual edifices concerning the issues of morality, they also have a tendency to ignore or to forget the practices to which these theories must finally be connected. As Kant himself puts it,

> the most remarkable thing about ordinary reason in its practical concern is that it may have as much hope as any philosopher of hitting the mark. In fact, it is almost more certain to do so than the philosopher, because he has no principle which the common understanding lacks, while his judgement is easily confused by a mass of irrelevant

---

[2]*KPR*, 5:172-73; Beck, p. 164.

considerations, so that it easily turns aside from the correct way.[3]

The problem commonly lost in a "mass of irrelevant considerations" is the problem of how one is to obey the moral law once one has first admired it.

It is probably reasonable to assume that the reason there is little written on the problem of obedience in Kant's moral philosophy is that this problem is usually dealt with separately in two other traditions of scholarship, the one legal and the other religious. Legal scholars frequently occupy themselves with problems concerning the efficacy of legal sanctions with powers to coerce exact proper civic conduct from the subjects of a political state.[4] Thus the problem of obedience reduces finally to the problem of the kind of policing necessary in that state. A coercive legal system is, therefore, a system of punitive external incentives or in some cases privileges. In a later section of this chapter, some of Kant's views of such systems in the light of his moral philosophy will be discussed.

Religious scholars, on the other hand, have for centuries addressed the problem of obedience in a slightly different, though analogous way. They have dealt with the problem of obedience either by supposing a powerful system of internal sanctions originating in some supernature, personal or impersonal, or by insisting upon the attractive power of God's promise of rewards for the pure in heart.[5] Some have argued that the doctrines of heaven and hell are themselves the motivators of righteous conduct.[6] Still others have insisted exclusively upon what might be called the affective power of God's love.[7]

---

[3]*Grundlegung*, 4:261; Beck, p. 21.

[4]Cf. Joel Feinberg & Hyman Gross, *Philosophy of Law* (Belmont, California: Dickenson Publishing Company, 1975). See especially chapter 5.

[5]Cf. Roland H. Bainton, *The Reformation of the Sixteenth Century* (Boston: The Beacon Press, 1952). See especially chapters 12 and 13.

[6]Cf. William Hordern, *Living by Grace* (Philadelphia: Wadsworth, 1977).

[7]Ibid.

Philosophers, though, have tended to regard both the legal and the religious solutions to the problem of obedience as solutions designed rather to circumvent the problem than to solve it. The moral man needs neither to be policed into doing his duty by a powerful state, nor induced to do it either by threat of damnation or promise of salvation.

One of the consequences of philosophers' reluctance to adopt the insights of the legal and religious solutions to the problem of obedience is that they have tended to neglect the problem altogether, naively assuming that casuistical meditations on the various moral truths or examinations of the language of morals would eliminate the need to address the problem of obedience. Perhaps it has also been assumed that philosophers, whose privileged status among the learned is generally acknowledged, have the right, and perhaps even the duty, to leave the problems of *application* to the empirical psychologists whose discipline "is not yet so rich as to be able to form a subject of study by itself, and yet is too important to be entirely excluded and forced to settle elsewhere, in a neighborhood that might well prove much less congenial than that of metaphysics."[8]

Kant's moral philosophy, as will be shown, deals with the problem of obedience first in the doctrine of moral judgment and secondly in the doctrine of the discipline of pure reason. The argument proceeds through several stages in this chapter. The argument begins by introducing the doctrine of judgment as it appears in *The Critique of Pure Reason*. The purpose here is to raise questions concerning the completeness of Kant's notion of judgment as the subsumption of particulars under universal rules. Kant argues that, though determinate procedures guide judgment in the production of experience, there can be no such procedures for the guidance of judgment where judgment is regarded as the activity of self-consciously applying theory to practice. The contention herein is that judgments in moral settings are really more than just the subsumption of particulars under universals. Judgments in moral contexts usually are self-judgments which are at the same time creative of moral attitudes and perspectives through which the moral dimensions of experience are forced into the foreground to become the matters of primary concern.

---

[8]*KI*, A848; B876.

The argument is roughly this: since Kant distinguishes between two different kinds of judgment in the first *Critique*, each is a different kind of activity. The categories are schematized in one, and empirical concepts are generated in the other. The former is an activity that proceeds in accordance with the determinate rules of "transcendental logic"; the latter is guided by what Kant calls a "discipline." "Discipline" is needed where there is no schematism to prevent an activity from going astray. This latter kind of judgment requires a special self-consciously managed thinking that the former does not. Judgments of the self-conscious sort proceed, therefore, with the guidance of discipline alone. This effort of judgment for which there can be no rules, is, it is argued, analogous to the effort expended in making moral judgments. What operates as a corrective for judgment is not the productive imagination's schemata but an array of subjective constraints which together Kant calls a *discipline*.

The thesis in this chapter is, therefore, that the central subjective feature of moral life is a sort of self-discipline, whose purpose it is to unite moral theory to moral practice for which there can be no rules which are exhaustive or determinate. The stability of moral life is produced by cautionary subjective hindrances whose origins are the moral laws themselves. These subjective hindrances are moral feelings.

It is crucial at this point to clarify this thesis before I support it textually. The discipline of judgment is not charged with the task of formulating moral principles. Pure feelings are not the sources of obligation—they are rather the pointers to it. Moral law is for Kant the source of obligation. Judgment is charged with the difficult task of wedding theory to practice by means of a discipline whose principal functions are to insure that moral laws are recognized, respected, and obeyed. The incentives of practical reason operate in this capacity.

Judgment in the *Critique of Pure Reason*

In the *Critique of Pure Reason* Kant offers his readers explicit accounts of judgment in three places: in section one of the "Analytic of Concepts" (A68-76; B93-101), in Book 2 of the "Transcendental Analytic" (A131-36; B169-75), and finally in chapter one of the "Transcendental Doctrine of Judgment" entitled "The Schematism of the Pure Concepts of Understanding" (A137-47; B176-87). Considering the difficulties of this doctrine the passages dealing with it are remarkably brief. After all, judgment is, according to Kant, nothing less than that activity of the understanding which subsumes particulars under the pure concepts of the understanding, thus uniting concepts with percepts in the production of experience. This activity is "the *application* of a category to appearances"[9] It is, Kant says, a function of unity. "By 'function'," he explains, "I mean the act of bringing various representations under one common representation."[10]

Kant's doctrine of judgment, as it appears in the first *Critique*, is then a doctrine spelling out the relationship between particulars and universals. The relationship between these two things must be mediated by some "third thing, which is homogeneous on the one hand with the category, and on the other hand with the appearance, and which thus makes the application of the former to the latter possible."[11] This third thing must be "void of all empirical content, and yet at the same time, while it must in one respect be *intellectual*, it must in another be *sensible*."[12] This third thing Kant calls the *transcendental schema* which is "a transcendental determination of time."[13]

In the transcendental aesthetic Kant had shown that time is one of the two forms of sensible intuition. Time he calls "inner sense" and space he calls "outer sense." The intent here, for purposes which subsequently will become clear, is to note some of the difficulties with Kant's account of time as the third thing which unites concepts with percepts. These difficulties are familiar philosophical ones: namely, the difficulties of unifying the non-temporal with the temporal.

In the first *Critique* Kant is attempting to account for the fact that we have experience at all. How is this experience possible? His answer, briefly, is that the categories of the understanding precondition and make possible the union of concepts and percepts. But the problem is that these two things are quite different. That they ultimately get

---

[9] *KI*, A138; B177.

[10] *KI*, A68; B93.

[11] *KI*, A138; B177.

[12] *KI*, A138; B177.

[13] *KI*, A138; B177.

united is clear from the fact that we have experience. What is of interest is the question of how they are united. The third thing which unites them, Kant claims, is something which is common to both concepts and percepts. This thing is produced, it seems, by an act of judgment. Kant calls it a *schema*. A schema is a transcendental determination of time. It is something which is both intellectual and sensible, yet void of all empirical content. This seems to be an unusual item in the inventory of Kantian discoveries.

Though no claim is made here to give a satisfactory account of the doctrine of the schematism, it is important for what will be argued in other sections of this chapter to provide some sort of description of the "action" of the schemata. The claim is only that the account of the schemata is imaginative and tailored to the problems which will be addressed in sections dealing with the wedding of theory to practice. It will be argued that the action of the schemata is analogous to the action of wedding moral theory to practice, in that very special efforts are required which can themselves be given only vaguely suggestive descriptions rather than either definitions or explanations. This is because the whole doctrine of judgment in Kant's work is shrouded in a mystery of sorts. It will become clear that this mystery is a very convenient one, for without it the very effort that is required of the person who chooses to live the moral life—an effort which, it is argued, is one of the most important aspects of that life—would be lost along with morality itself.

One way to describe the action of schemata would be to say that they discharge the responsibilities given them by the understanding of slowing down percepts as they speed by just long enough for them to be imprisoned for awhile. They must, that is, first be apprehended. Next they are comprehended. Comprehension could be likened to the "booking" under a rule of law of previously fleeing percepts. Once they are "booked" they can then be released on parole and ordered never again to be wayward. Booking, or comprehension, consists of the conditioning of the percepts by the categories of the understanding. Experience is possible, we might say, just to the extent that the schemata are able to regiment the lives of percepts in accordance with conditioning rules of law. The schemata can be thought of as deputies of sorts, living half-way between the eternal world of law and the seamy world of crime. Their responsibilities are to deliver as best they can the chaotic from their lives as outlaws to a more harmonious existence in a community of rules.

Experience is itself testimony to the fact that this job gets done. What is remarkable about it is that in all of its complexity to us it seems quite effortless. This effortlessness is surprising even to Kant, because he is aware of the difficulties involved in trying to account for the harmony of our cognitive faculties with the perceptual world. The tasking of the schematism outlined in his transcendental logic is "the correcting and securing of judgment, by means of determinate rules, in the use of the pure understanding."[14] The function of the schematism is recognized by Kant to be a "peculiar one"[15] likened to an *art*.

> This schematism of our understanding, in its application to appearances and their mere form, is an art concealed in the depths of the soul, whose real modes of activity nature is hardly likely ever to allow us to discover, and to have open to our gaze.[16]

Even though "determinate rules" task the schematism, a truth discovered in transcendental logic, the method by which the schematism enforces the rules is an "art concealed in the depths of the soul."

The application of a category to appearances is effected by the schematism whose "real modes of activity" are undiscovered. What can be known is that the wedding of categories to appearances does take place, and that the wedding is a sort of ceremony effected by *transcendental judgment*. But transcendental judgments differ from the judgments of general logic. The former are effortless, the latter are not. The determinate rules of transcendental logic "correct and secure" judgment in its transcendental employment. That is why such judgments are effortless. Judgments in general logic get no such rules for guidance and are, therefore, not determinately corrected or secured. When we are forced to make judgments we are quite aware of this lack of guidance. We experience something of a struggle to make

---

[14]*KI*, A135; B174.

[15]*KI*, A135; B174.

[16]*KI*, A141; B180-81.

correct judgments in the absence of "rules for judgment."[17]

Kant's first mention of this difficulty in the *Critique of Pure Reason* is lengthy but worth quoting at length. He writes:

> General logic contains, and can contain, no rules for judgment. . . . If it sought to give general instructions how we are to subsume under these rules, that is, to distinguish whether something does or does not come under them, that could only be by means of another rule. This, in turn, for the very reason that it is a rule, again demands guidance from judgment. And thus it appears that, though understanding is capable of being instructed, and of being equipped with rules, judgment is a peculiar talent which can be practiced only, and cannot be taught. It is the specific quality of so-called mother-wit; and its lack no school can make good.[18]

Kant is worried here about an infinite regress. It appears that if judgment sought rules for subsuming particulars under concepts, more rules would be sought for the application of those, and so on. It seems to follow then that those people who are good judges possess a "peculiar talent." It is peculiar because they are able to judge correctly in the *absence of rules*, or in the absence of obvious methods guiding their judgment. The talent of judging, "so-called mother-wit," cannot be taught because there are no rules to teach, or because where there are rules to teach there is no guarantee that they will not be wrongly employed.

> For although an abundance of rules borrowed from the insight of others may be grafted upon a limited understanding, the power of rightly employing them must belong to the learner himself; and in the absence of such a natural gift no rule that may be prescribed to him for this purpose can ensure against misuse.[19]

At this point in his discussion Kant provides his readers with examples to illustrate what he means when he says that judgment is a

---

[17]*KI*, A133; B172.

[18]*KI*, A132-33; B171-72.

[19]*KI*. A133-34; B172-73.

natural talent the lack of which "no school can make good."

> A physician, a judge, or a ruler may have at command many
> excellent pathological, legal, or political rules, even to the
> degree that he may become a profound teacher of them, and
> yet, nonetheless, may easily stumble in their application.
> For, although admirable in understanding, he may be
> wanting in the natural power of judgment. He may
> comprehend the universal *in abstracto*, and yet not be able
> to distinguish whether a case *in concreto* comes under it. Or
> the error may be due to his not having received, through
> examples and actual practice, adequate training for this
> particular act of judgment.[20]

Kant is talking about people whose judgment is deficient primarily
because of a lack of experience, practice and examples. He warns his
readers, though, that examples used to "sharpen judgment" may and
often do impair "correctness and precision of intellectual insight."[21]
The problem with examples is that they

> only very seldom . . . adequately fulfill the requirements of
> the rule (as *casus in terminus*). Besides, they often weaken
> that effort which is required of the understanding to
> comprehend properly the rules in their universality, in
> independence of the particular circumstances of experience,
> and so accustom us to use rules rather as formulas than as
> principles. Examples are thus the go-cart of judgment; and
> those who are lacking in the natural talent can never
> dispense with them.[22]

There are mentioned in Kant's work two different kinds of people
in whom the talent for judging is either deficient or absent. The one
who is deficient in this talent and is accustomed to use "rules rather as
formulas than as principles" is the *pedant. The one who seems to lack
this talent altogether is the one Kant calls stupid.* In a footnote Kant
says, "deficiency in judgment is just what is ordinarily called stupidity,

---

[20]*KI*, A134; B173-74.

[21]*KI*, A134; B173-74

[22]*KI*, A134; B173-74.

and for such a failing there is no remedy."²³ I am here making the distinction a sharper one than Kant does in order to claim that pedantry, though certainly a deficiency, is to some extent remediable and thus a mere deficiency, while stupidity should be considered an absence for which there is no remedy.

A pedant may well misuse rules, but he is often able to understand them *in abstracto*. A stupid person lacks judgment usually because he cannot understand them at all. Kant's discussion of pedantry in the *Logic* differs from his discussion of stupidity in the *Critique*. An examination of the former should bring some clarity to the issues I am raising at this point.²⁴

In the introduction to the *Logic*, Kant lists three main sources of prejudices: imitation, habit, and inclination. Imitation, he says, is the tendency ". . . for taking as true what others have alleged as true."²⁵ Significantly the *habit* of *imitation*, Kant says, can hardly be cured. This habit of imitation, Kant says, "may also be called a *propensity for the passive use of reason*, or for the *mechanism of reason instead of its spontaneity under laws*."²⁶ It is the "laziness of so many men (that) makes them tread in the footsteps of others rather than exert the powers of their own understanding."²⁷ The imitator, according to Kant, is a man too lazy to use his own mind properly and who seeks to avoid such irksome work by imitating the genuine work of others. He is always, therefore, looking for shortcuts.

The most familiar shortcut to "tread in" is the *formula*. Imitators have the tiresome habit of using "rules rather as formulas than as principles."²⁸ A formula is defined in the *Logic* as a rule "whose expression serves as a pattern for imitation."²⁹ It is clear that the search

---

²³*KI*, B173n.

²⁴The notion of pedantry is discussed in later parts of this chapter and in chapter five of this essay.

²⁵*Logik*, 8:386; Hartmann, p. 84.

²⁶*Logik*, 8:387; Hartmann, p. 84.

²⁷Ibid.

²⁸*KI*, A134; B173.

²⁹*Logik*, 8:387; Hartmann, p. 85.

for a rule to imitate is itself an indication of deficiency in judgment. The tendency of most men, Kant is suggesting, is to substitute for thought some easily copied formula, thus making use of their reason in a merely passive and mechanical way rather than making use of it intelligently. The substitution of a formula for thinking amounts to the making of a *judgment without reflecting*.[30] And the person most clearly guilty of this is the pedant.

Kant's portrait of the pedant in the *Logic*, presented here in its entirety, is both entertaining and illuminating.

> The pedant is either, as the man of learning, set off against the man of the world and insofar is the arrogant erudite without knowledge of the world, i.e., without knowing how to communicate his science to others; or he is to be considered as the man of skill, but only in *formalities*, not as to essence and ends. In the latter meaning he picks at formalities and is narrow-minded in respect of the core of things, looking only to the dress and the shell. He is the unsuccessful imitator or *caricature* of a *methodical* man. One may therefore also call pedantry a ruminating fastidiousness and useless exactitude (micrology) in matters of form. . .
>
> A purposeful exactness in matters of form is *thoroughness* (scholastic perfection). Pedantry is thus an *affectation* of thoroughness, just as galanterie is a mere pandering to the plaudits of taste, nothing but an affectation of popularity. . .
>
> To avoid pedantry there is required wide knowledge not only in the sciences themselves but also in respect of their use. Only the truly learned man can therefore free himself from pedantry, which is always the property of a narrow mind.[31]

Kant seems never to tire of criticizing the pedant. His figure is found in many of Kant's works, which suggests that Kant regarded

---

[30] *Logik*, 8:386; Hartmann, p. 84.

[31] *Logik*, 8:362; Hartmann, pp. 51-52.

him to be formidably pathological. Later in the *Anthropology*[32] Kant represents him as a man who can learn but who cannot think.

> A man who can learn a great deal but cannot *think for himself* is said to have a *limited* (narrow) mind.—A man can be *enormously* erudite (a machine for teaching others in the same way he was taught), and yet be very *limited* when it comes to using his historical knowledge rationally.—A man whose way of handling what he has learned, when he communicates publicly, betrays the constraint of the school (and so a want of freedom in thinking for himself) is a *pedant*, whether he is a scholar, a soldier, or even a courtier. Of these, the scholarly pedant is the most tolerable, because we can learn from him. On the other hand, the soldier's or courtier's scrupulous observance of formalities (pedantry) is not only useless but ridiculous, because here the inevitable pride of the pedant is that of an *ignoramus*.[33]

In a later section of the *Anthropology* in the midst of a rather lengthy discussion of wit, Kant returns to the pedant describing him this time in language mirroring that of the description in the *Logic*.[34] "Wit in playing with words is *insipid*," Kant writes, "while futile subtlety (micrology) of judgment is *pedantic*."[35]

The point to be made here, on the basis of the sketches of the pedant just presented, is that pedantry in judgment is the tendency to create useless, futile, oversubtle formulae for the application of principles where what is required instead is the spontaneous or intelligent use of reason. It is also clearly the tendency to invent *schemata*, for example, of rank,[36] where none is appropriate.

The whole point of Kant's discussion of the absence of rules for the use of judgment is that the natural talent, mother-wit, spontaneity of

---

[32]In Kant's *Anthropologie* there is presented a whole catalogue of strange characters.

[33]*Anthropologie*, 8:23; Gregor, p. 19.

[34]*Logik*, 8:386-87; Hartmann, pp. 84-85.

[35]*Anthropologie*, 8:111; Gregor, p. 90.

[36]*Anthropologie*, 8:212-13; Gregor, pp. 180-81.

reason, or whatever we choose to call it, takes the place of *schemata* in moral judgments. The pedant is one who is the servant of intellectual mechanisms created either by himself or by others to fill in a gap appropriately bridged only by the original and creative efforts of clear, and to be sure, irksome, thinking. What is characteristic of this thinking is that it must proceed without the help of *schemata*, yet according to Kant, it is a thinking guided by laws. He contrasts "the passive use of reason," and "the mechanism of reason" with "its spontaneity under laws."[37]

Moral judgments differ from ordinary perceptual judgments in several interesting and important ways. Moral judgments consist of the estimation *(Beurteilung)* of the extent to which maxims satisfy the demands of the moral law for universality. It is easy to oversimplify this process (a common mistake of interpreters of Kant's work) by supposing it amounts to the application of a rigid procedure which in itself guarantees a determinate outcome. This is the mistake of the moral pedant. It is not just that moral judgments are, in fact, the products of a much richer thinking process, but that they *ought to be*. Ordinary perceptual judgments, for example, that an object is a chair, or that the background of a painting is blue, and so forth, require, except for perceptual novices, little, if any, imaginative effort. One simply subsumes the object under determinate rules of judgment—the empirical concepts of chairs and blue backgrounds are schematized.

What this means is that the judgments that familiar objects are such and such are judgments based upon linguistically conditioned habits of thought. All that is required is a simple act of subsumption. Moral judgments differ in that there are no habits of thought upon which an agent is able to rely. A moral agent must first construct in the imagination an ectypal world in which his maxim could be a *natural* law. The question is not whether a given maxim could be universalized within the parochial social context of his own community, but whether it could be universalized in the context of a possible moral community—within at least one of several possible ideals of the Kingdom of Ends.

Ordinary cognitive judgments require no such imaginative effort. The world in which familiar objects exist does not need to be imagined,

---

[37] *Logik*, 8:386-87; Hartmann, pp. 84-85.

because it is habitually given. The moral world, since it is not perceptually given, must be first conceptualized. There is, consequently, a kind of underdetermination infecting moral judgments which cannot, normally, infect perceptual judgments. This underdetermination is systemic. Moral judgments usually require decisions to be made, not simply subsumptions. Their justifications usually, therefore, include the careful articulation of the imaginative context in which the maxim is harmonious—a world in which it *has been universalized*.

These differ from scientific-theoretical judgments in that the end of moral judgments is action, the end of scientific-theoretical judgments is the verification of a hypothesis. The moral agent runs risks, therefore, which are not usual for persons-as-perceivers or for persons-as-scientists. An example of the imaginative construction of a possible world as the context in which moral judgments are made might help to clarify the points I have been making above.

A story is told of one of Queen Victoria's court jesters. He was walking down one of those filthy London streets when he had the opportunity to settle a dispute between a beggar and an owner of a cookshop. The beggar had been sitting in front of the cookshop so he could enjoy the smell of a roast cooking while he was eating his bread. The shop owner, seeing the beggar, demanded that he pay for the aroma of the roast. The beggar refused. The dispute became quite heated. The court jester, acting as a moral arbiter, settled the dispute by insisting that the beggar pay for the *aroma* of the roast with the *sound* of his money. The two disputants agreed that such was an intelligent solution to the problem.

The example, though trivial to be sure, illustrates, nonetheless, that in the absence of a determinate procedure for settling the dispute—the moral problem—a world in which aromas and sounds stand on an equal footing, that is, are equally valuable, and in which an interesting sort of social reciprocity is the supreme moral norm, was constructed to form a context in which the two disputants could reconcile their differences. How else could such a problem be resolved? Such, I think, is the case with many of the moral judgments we are forced to make. A world in which a problem can be resolved must first be constructed, because one does not preexist. It is the mistake of the moral pedant to suppose that the preexisting social conventions provide what context is needed to solve most moral disputes. He searches, therefore, for simple formulae—patterns of judgment, Kant says, which can be easily imitated.

Pedantry is, therefore, the tendency to defeat the spontaneous and creative efforts of reason in making judgments by substituting for those efforts a mere *mechanism of thought*. A pedant is one who habitually substitutes mechanical thinking—a kind of calculation—for genuine thought and thus becomes a slave to those ways of thinking which are peculiarly effortless and usually fruitless. Pedants are, accordingly, intellectually servile. Their judgments are sterile attempts to avoid the "core" of things. When it comes to moral matters this tendency to avoid genuine thinking produces a person with a *defective character*.

A pedant in moral matters is a person who misses the *spirit* of the law by enslaving himself to its *letter*.[38] The pedant can be expected to be a scrupulous observer of all of the moral conventions. Morality, for the pedant, is at best a propriety designed carefully to spare him censure. Genuine morality is thus lost in a "mass of irrelevancies."[39]

Kant's Notion of Discipline

If the creation of formulae—pedantry—does not fulfill the requirements for the correcting and securing of judgment in its practical employment, and if there are no rules to guide it, then what does Kant offer in his doctrine of judgment to take the place of *schemata*? Something must connect moral theory to moral practice. Surely he did not leave this important matter to the preachers of his day. I shall argue here that Kant's doctrine of the *discipline of reason* supplies his moral philosophy with the bridge between theory and practice. To begin I shall introduce Kant's discussion of discipline as it is found in the later sections of the *Critique of Pure Reason*.[40]

Kant's use of the term "discipline" is restricted in his critical works to its negative meanings:

---

[38] *KPR*, 5:80; Beck, p. 75.

[39] *Grundlegung*, 4:261; Beck, p. 21.

[40] *KI*, "The Discipline of Pure Reason," A709-94; B737-822.

I am well aware that in the terminology of the schools the title *discipline* is commonly used as synonymous with instruction. However, there are so many other cases where discipline in the sense of *training by constraint* is carefully distinguished from instruction in the sense of *teaching*, and the very nature of things itself makes it so imperative that we should preserve the only expressions suitable for this distinction, that it is desirable that the former term should never be used in any but the negative sense.[41]

Training by constraint, then, is what Kant means by discipline. Such training is necessary "where the limits of our possible knowledge are very narrow, where the temptation to judge is great, where illusion that besets us is very deceptive and the harm that results from error is considerable."[42] Most significant for the present is the following statement:

The compulsion, by which the constant tendency to disobey certain rules is restrained and finally extirpated, we entitle *discipline*. It is distinguished from *culture*, which is intended solely to give a certain kind of skill, and not to cancel any habitual mode of action already present. Towards the development of a talent, which has already in itself an impulse to manifest itself, discipline will therefore contribute in a negative, culture and doctrine in a positive, fashion.[43]

Training by constraint, discipline, is needed in these important areas: (1) where there is a tendency (we might say inclination) to disobey certain rules, (2) where there are bad habits that need to be destroyed or transformed, and (3) where a talent beginning to manifest itself can be further developed by preventing it from collapsing.

It is quite clear from the arguments in "The Discipline of Pure Reason"[44] that Kant considers his own critical philosophy to be an

---

[41]*KI*, A711; B739.

[42]*KI*, A709; B737.

[43]*KI*, A709-710; B737-38.

[44]See note 40 above.

example of philosophy (perhaps the only philosophy) genuinely disciplined by reason. Critical philosophy, in Kant's sense, is designed first to discover the *limits* of human knowledge and secondly to restrict and confine our cognitive claims to the bounds of possible experiences. It is likewise clear that the deeper wisdom guiding human conduct in the practical sphere, according to Kant, is cautionary rather than hortatory. The problem facing the person attempting to be moral is primarily that of forcing himself to obey what he knows to be his duties once he has become even vaguely aware of them. Few people complain of the effort it takes to yield to the currents of nature.

It is Kant's view that most men's lives can be characterized by a continuing surrender to a distressing array of temptations. What is called for here is constraint in the form of self-control. He has argued that it takes no special talent for men to become aware of their duties, but that it takes a tremendous effort to fulfill them. Something, therefore, must serve to constrain them to do their duties. If there were no constraining incentives generated by the moral law men would at the most merely contemplate it, going on about their lives in totally unregenerate ways.

There is a complication here that must be noted. It certainly takes discipline to obey the laws we once acknowledge, but it takes discipline also to continue to acknowledge them in their formal purity. So discipline in morality serves first to secure a lasting attentiveness (*Beachtung*) to the laws, and secondly it constrains us to obey them. It is certainly true, according to Kant, that in moral matters, especially, there is a "tendency to disobey certain rules," there are "bad habits that need to be destroyed," and there is a gradually developing talent manifesting itself first in the recognition of duties which needs discipline for its development.[45]

On Self-Mastery and Morality

Kant's moral theory can now be seen to consist of at least three separate but related doctrinal parts: (1) the categorical imperative and the duties derivable from it, that is, a formal a priori system of laws, (2) a doctrine of motivation consisting of the incentives arising from those

---

[45]See note 43 above.

laws, and (3) a discipline consisting of "a system of precautions and self-examination,"[46] whose function is to "liberate the will from the despotism of desires, whereby, in our attachment to certain natural things, we are rendered incapable of exercising a choice of our own."[47] This discipline is erected primarily to insure against incorrect practice and poor judgment.

It is Kant's view, I urge, that once moral theory has been grounded in a priori laws, a task assigned exclusively to philosophy, the key to correct practice is not to be found already articulated in a casuistry of sorts. In a sense there is no *key* to correct practice, because correct practice is the product of a long and difficult therapy which is generated and reinforced by incentives in the form of subjective constraints arising in the very recognition of those laws.

As has already been mentioned in chapter one, there are, according to Kant, two sources of motivation competing for sovereignty: the inclinations and the moral laws. Discipline serves to suppress the former so that the latter can ascend to its rightful dominance, after which it generates the constraints preventing the person now attentive to the moral laws from stumbling in their application. The correct application of moral theory to practice is, therefore, the product of that discipline, personalized in Kant's writings often as "a fully matured judgment."[48]

It is perhaps necessary to raise on behalf of those suspicious of the argument thus far a few questions about it, in hopes of resolving a problem that may seem to have been conveniently overlooked. The problem of the application of moral principles to practice is dealt with already in the four examples of the *Groundwork*. Why then insist that Kant's account of practice is contained in his doctrine of discipline? There are two replies to this question.

First, the central concern of the *Groundwork* is the formal justification and explanation of the categorical imperative. Kant's

---

[46]*K1*, A711; B739.

[47]*K3*, 5:511-12; Meredith, p. 95. See pages 95ff. for a discussion of discipline. See paragraph 83, part 2, for a more lengthy discussion of discipline.

[48]*K1*, A761; B789.

effort is to supply a "Groundwork of the Metaphysics of Morals," rather than to supply a manual for moral practice. We cannot therefore expect Kant to have given any but brief suggestions, that is, examples of practice, more to flesh out the content of the moral law than to teach readers how to apply it. Secondly, even though Kant does give examples of the application of the moral law in a few particular cases in the *Groundwork* and further extends the scope of examples in the *Metaphysic of Morals*, [49] where he is obviously concerned with the whole array of perfect and imperfect duties, there is still left over the problem of how to fulfill the spirit of these laws as well as the letter of them.

It is evident from all of Kant's moral writings that, should a person be fully conscious of what his duties are, even down to the most minute ones, given an external system of sanctions, it is still possible for him outwardly to appear to have fulfilled his obligations while in fact he has not. That is, he could live in complete accordance or conformity with the moral laws without respecting them. His actions, though legal, may not be moral. Thus there is a more profound problem Kant is attempting to address in his doctrine of discipline. The problem is not just how to persuade persons to live in accordance with moral laws, for there are many ways to enforce adherence to them, but rather how one is to discipline oneself to respect and to obey them.

This problem is addressed frontally in two of Kant's later works.[50] It arises as the question of what it means to say to someone that he is his own master. The moral man, the man acting for the sake of the law and not just in accordance with it, satisfies in practice the demands that his act be both legal and moral. A brief consideration of Kant's notion of self-mastery will, perhaps, make this issue clearer.

Citizenship and Mastery

In the 1793 essay on *Theory and Practice*[51] there is a section in which Kant is attempting to state the necessary qualifications for

---

[49] *Metaphysik der Sitten in zwei Teilen* (1797), 7. *The Metaphysical Principles of Virtue*, trans. by James Ellington (New York: Bobbs-Merrill, 1964). Hereafter cited as *Tugendlehre*.

[50] *Theorie und Praxis*, 6, and *Aufklärung*, 4.

[51] *Theorie und Praxis*, 6.

citizenship in a state. First among these qualifications, Kant insists, is that a man be *his own master*. The reason for this requirement, so important to Kant, is that the person who is his own master is not the servant of others and consequently cannot be used by them for ends inconsistent with the laws of the community at large. The person who is his own master is a person who owns, Kant says, some sort of property so that he can live "only by *disposing* of what is *his own*."[52]

In a footnote to this passage Kant distinguishes between landowners and people who own property in a broader sense.[53] A person owns his work (*opus*) if he can "convey it to another by transfer." The question arises: does a day-laborer, who is unskilled, own anything such that he could be considered for full citizenship? Can he ever qualify as a master of himself, since he so obviously depends upon others for his living?[54] Interestingly and uncharacteristically, Kant concludes his footnote with this sentence: "It is, I confess, somewhat difficult to determine just what it takes to be able to claim the status of being one's own master."[55]

It is uncharacteristic of Kant here to admit difficulties, because in other contexts, perhaps even less clear ones, Kant confidently asserts what it means to be one's own master. In the *Enlightenment* essay of 1784 Kant is unequivocal about this matter.[56] Enlightenment, Kant argues here, is a matter of having the courage and resolution to make use of one's understanding without direction from another. Tutelage, he says, "is man's inability to make use of his understanding without direction from another."[57] A man is his own master, it seems, when he makes free and courageous use of his own mind in matters that concern not only himself but also his fellows.

An ideal citizen would obviously be someone who is enlightened in Kant's sense. I believe the difficulty expressed in the *Theory and*

---

[52] *Theorie und Praxis*, 6:379; Ashton, p. 63.

[53] *Theorie und Praxis*, 6:379n; Ashton, p. 63.

[54] Ibid.

[55] Ibid.

[56] *Aufklärung*, 4.

[57] *Aufklärung*,, 4:169; Beck, p. 85.

Practice essay is a result of Kant's reluctance to identify "being one's own master" with either one's occupation or property, because he knows (1) that enlightenment should be possible for everyone,[58] and (2) that it is ownership of one's own mind,[59] so to speak, that distinguishes a free man from a slave, and not his other possessions or skills.

Nevertheless, Kant is keenly aware of the realities of politics: that people who are financially indebted to others, or whose livelihoods depend on "gracious lords," are often in fact "placid creatures" who would "not dare take a step without the harness of the cart to which they are tethered."[60] This is true because "the step to competence is held to be very dangerous by the far greater portion of mankind," to which Kant adds, "quite apart from its being arduous."[61]

There is another problem to which Kant was probably attuned when he expressed difficulty in defining what it is to be one's own master. In *Perpetual Peace*,[62] Kant identifies the good citizen with the person who obeys the laws of the state. A good citizen is a servant of the political order, but he need not be morally enlightened. In fact, it is possible for a devil to be a good citizen, given a system of laws with sanctions powerful enough to force him to obey.

> The problem of organizing a state, however hard it may seem, can be solved even for a race of devils if only they are intelligent.[63]

---

[58]*Aufklärung*, 4:170; Beck, p. 86. Cf. *K1*, A836; B859.

[59]Cf. *K1*, A836; B864, for a discussion of differences between rational and historical knowledge and for a contrast similar to the one discussed here.

[60]*Aufklärung*, 4:169; Beck, p. 85. The German here reads: "*die ruhigen Geschöpfen.*"

[61]Ibid.

[62]*Zum ewigen Frieden: Ein philosophischen Entwurf* (1794), 6. *Perpetual Peace* in *On History*, edited and trans. by Lewis White Beck (New York: Bobbs-Merrill, 1963). Hereafter cited as *Perpetual Peace*.

[63]*Perpetual Peace*, 6:452; Beck, p. 112: "*Das Problem der Staatserrichtung ist, so hart wie es auch klingt, selbst für ein Volk von Teufeln (wenn sie nur Verstand haben) . . . .*"

A devil here is simply someone who "is secretly inclined to exempt himself"[64] from the laws that are necessary for the preservation of a state, but who is nevertheless intelligent enough to respond to pressures which, if applied properly in the right places, would exact from him public conduct appearing to others as if it had arisen from other than "evil intentions."[65]

There is a restricted and non-moral sense, therefore, of the term "good citizen" and consequently a restricted sense of "being one's own master." Given a state peopled only by devils, those in it qualifying for citizenship would be those most directly responsive to the sovereign, that is, those whose possessions, either of property or skill, would free them from the slavery of want for service to the larger community and its laws. They can be pressured to serve others unwillingly, because the only master they fear and hence obey is the sovereign himself. A "good citizen" is, in the restricted sense, an "enlightened" egoist.

In the first sense a master of himself is simply one whose conduct appears to be good because he is pressured to conduct himself legally in a state where the laws are rational and universal. In the second sense a master of himself is a moral man. His conduct not only appears to be good, but is good. It is not merely legal, but moral. He is a master of himself not because he owes political allegiance to no one, but because he is not a slave of his inclinations. His actions are not motivated primarily by his desire for happiness, but by his respect for the moral law. Unlike the enlightened devil who is free only to obey the laws of the state, the moral man is free to obey moral laws of his own making.

In the language of the *Groundwork* Kant makes the distinction between the actions of the enlightened devil and the moral man by saying that the former acts *heteronomously* and the latter *autonomously*.[66] The former obeys laws of another; the latter obeys his own laws.

As Kant had noted, the problem of exacting good conduct is not too difficult, given an effective system of legal sanctions. But conduct

---

[64]Ibid.

[65]Ibid. The German text reads: "*böse Gesinnungen.*"

[66]*Grundlegung*, 4:299ff.; Beck, p. 59ff.

that appears to be good may not in fact be moral. The question I am raising is this: by what practices does Kant believe it is possible for an heteronomous man to become autonomous? How are demons to be transformed into moral individuals?[67]

The problem, as I said earlier, is really a profound one. Suppose, for example, that I've chosen to do what is right in a particular case. It is one thing to discover what is right, that is, what accords with the moral law. (Testimony to the fact that this is not always easy to determine is the immense literature now available on the categorical imperative and its applications.)[68] It is quite another to perform that act morally. For how do we purify our own incentives? How can we make certain that our acts are not really inspired by secret impulses of self-love?[69] How can we ever free ourselves from the suspicion that we are ourselves demons acting as the servants of the inclinations?[70]

The demands of morality, according to Kant, far exceed the demands of citizenship. It is not enough for us to obey the law; we must obey it in the proper spirit.[71] The practice of morality consists therefore of a discipline intended to purify intentions.[72] This discipline is, we might say, spiritually therapeutic. Its purpose is nothing less than the transformation of character.[73]

---

[67]This may be an exaggerated way of stating the issue. Nevertheless, it is the way Kant discusses it in *Anthropology* and in *Religion*. It can be found discussed that way also in the *Groundwork* in a slightly disguised form. There the problem is how a good will is produced.

[68]Cf. Marcus Singer's *Generalization in Ethics* for one of the most thorough treatments of this topic. Of course, there is a vast literature dealing with this problem which cannot be dealt with here.

[69]Cf. *Grundlegung*, 4:264; Beck, p. 23.

[70]See also *Religion*, passim.

[71]Cf. *KPR*, 5:79-80; Beck pp. 74-75.

[72]What else could be the object of such practices? Conduct is not moral (it has no moral worth) unless the incentives driving it are moral ones. The problem is not how to exact proper conduct, but how to transform dispositions or attitudes.

[73]If we identify character with a settled arrangement of dispositions or attitudes, it follows that if we attempt to transform the latter we are also transforming the former.

As individuals we are charged with the duty of making ourselves good.[74] This can also be characterized as the duty to transform our own moral dispositions from bad to good.[75] The profound difficulties facing a person charged with such a responsibility can best be seen in a context considerably broader than that in which they are ordinarily discussed by Kant's many commentators.[76] The discipline of morality consists of far more than the determination of the moral correctness of outward acts or the checking of maxims. Kant's moral philosophy seen in a larger setting begins to appear less like a decision theory than, as Kroner[77] has called it, a *Weltanschauung.*

Moral self-discipline, for Kant, is, as it has already been argued,[78] the corrective for certain types of moral failure, particularly for failures in judgment. However, it is charged with more than the task of guiding judgment in the determination of worth of individual actions.[79] As will be shown below, moral self-discipline is principally a discipline[80] whose task is to transform character and to ensure the

---

[74]Cf. *Religion*, passim.

[75]See notes 72 and 73 above.

[76]Note especially those writers of articles who fail to mention or to notice the religious setting of Kant's moral philosophy. It is not argued that Kant's moral philosophy is itself religious, but that most of the crucial questions Kant raises are difficult to understand against any background other than a religious one. Perhaps the most insightful of works dealing with the religious background of Kant's day is Walter Benjamin's *The Origin of German Tragic Drama*, translated by John Osborne (London: NLB, 1977).

[77]Cf. Richard Kroner, *Kant's Weltanschauung* (Chicago: University of Chicago Press, 1956), passim. Suggested here is that Kant's moral philosophy is a study of a special way of seeing the world and that such seeing requires a continuous discipline.

[78]Though it is a corrective it is not a cure or a remedy. It is instead the name for a system of self-imposed constraints.

[79]Discipline is a corrective for certain types of moral failure due to the relaxation of moral attitudes: attitudes which precede and, therefore, color all conduct.

[80]That moral discipline is essentially self-discipline follows from the fact that its object is a person's own attitudes.

maintenance of moral attitudes.[81]

The notion of a moral attitude is introduced here as a substitute for what Kant calls a moral disposition. The pilgrimage of the moral man from bad to better is guided and prompted by this rigorous self-discipline; a discipline Kant himself regarded as "arduous" and "irksome,"[82] but nevertheless a necessary one.

This notion of a moral attitude is mentioned to emphasize again that the pilgrimage to moral perfection, or rather to moral betterment, is not simply a matter of making the correct moral choices one after another. There is *no* Kantian *methodology* for this pilgrimage.[83] In the *Anthropology from a Pragmatic Point of View*[84] there is a section in which Kant discusses briefly the transformation of character—or to use his terminology "the establishment of character."[85] In his language "having character" is the same as having a good character.[86] After giving a list[87] of the principles having to do with character, including (1) not intentionally to say what is false, (2) not to dissemble, (3) not to break our (legitimate) promises, (4) not to associate by preference with evil-minded men, and (5) to pay no attention to gossip, Kant offers his readers a description of character transformation.

> A man who is conscious of (having) character in his way of
> thinking does not have it by nature; he must always have
> *acquired* it. Since the act of establishing character, like a

---

[81]The notion of moral attitudes is used here in place of Kant's notion of dispositions or predispositions not to defeat Kant's distinction but to put the problem in the context in which it is ordinarily discussed by non-specialists. Most of us understand what is meant by an attitude—a particular way of thinking about a certain range of issues, or a posture vis-à-vis those issues.

[82]*Aufklärung*, 4 and Beck, passim. There is mention of the ardor of freeing oneself from tutelage.

[83]Here the word "methodology" is used as a term contrasting with "discipline." Both are rigorous, though the former can perhaps be articulated precisely and formally while the latter probably cannot.

[84]See note 32 above.

[85]*Anthropologie*, 8:187; Gregor, p. 159.

[86]*Anthropologie*, 8:184; Gregor, p. 157.

[87]*Anthropologie*, 8:186; Gregor, p. 159.

kind of rebirth, is a certain ceremony of making a vow to oneself, we may assume that the solemnity of the act makes it and the moment when the transformation took place unforgettable to him, like the beginning of a new epoch.[88]

External incentives cannot produce this transformation. He continues:

Education, examples and instruction cannot produce this firmness and steadfastness in our principles *gradually*, but only as it were, by an explosion that results from our being sick and tired of the precarious state of instinct. Perhaps there are but few who have attempted this revolution before the age of thirty, and fewer still who have consolidated it firmly before they are forty.[89]

The pilgrimage begins then as an explosion resulting in a *revolution*[90] or *rebirth* the consolidation of which takes *at least ten years*. Finally Kant has this to say about becoming a *better man*:

Wanting to become a better man in a fragmentary way is a futile endeavor, since the impression dies out while we are working on another; the act of establishing character, however, is absolute unity of the inner principle of our conduct generally.[91]

The point, it seems, is that though it is possible to perform one good act and then another, becoming a good man (or a better one) requires an *inner transformation* rather than the piecemeal performances of several good actions. The explosion representing the inner transformation of character then is really a self-induced catharsis purifying the ground of action. It is, in the language of the *Groundwork*, the production of a *good will*.[92]

---

[88]*Anthropologie*, 8:187; Gregor, p. 159.

[89]*Anthropologie,* 8:187; Gregor, p. 159.

[90]*Religion,* 6:187ff.; Greene, pp. 43ff.

[91]*Anthropologie*, 8:187; Gregor, p. 159.

[92]*Grundlegung*, 4:252; Beck, p. 12.

It is easy now to connect Kant's observation on character with moral discipline by citing one further passage, which in the *Anthropology* immediately precedes Kant's list of principles having to do with character.[93]

> Character requires maxims that proceed from reason and morally practical principles. So it is not correct to say that the evil in a certain man is a quality of his character; for in that case it would be diabolical. But man never sanctions the evil in himself, and so there is really no evil from principles; it comes only from abandoning principles.[94]

A man of character is one who has submitted himself to the constraints of moral laws, and who has done so freely in a single explosive act renouncing the evil in himself. What is left for him to do is to continue to struggle. It is in this context that discipline can clearly be seen to be a continuous moral *self-judgment* of the most rigorous sort.[95]

Moral self-judgment is, I urge, the primary task of moral judgment generally. It is clear that since moral self-judgment works as a constant check on the purity of intentions, that is, on the moral character of one's self, such judgment cannot be made on others simply for the reason that the moral quality of their intentions is not open to our inspection.[96] Hence, moral judgment, in the strictest sense, is self-judgment.[97]

Perhaps the clearest of Kant's statements on self-judgment is found in the *Metaphysics of Morals*, paragraph 13:

> Every man has a conscience and finds himself observed by an internal judge, who threatens him and keeps him in awe (respect combined with fear). This authority watching over

---

[93]*Anthropologie*, 8:186; Gregor, p. 159.

[94]Ibid.

[95]Cf. Milton C. Nahm, " 'Sublimity' and the 'Moral Law' in Kant's Philosophy," *Kant-Studien* 48:1-4 (1956-1957): 502ff.

[96]Cf. *Grundlegung*, 4, passim; Beck, passim.

[97]Cf. Nahm, " 'Sublimity' and the 'Moral Law'."

the laws within him is not something which he himself (arbitrarily) creates, but is incorporated in his being. If he tries to run away, his conscience follows him like his shadow. To be sure, he can stupefy himself with pleasures and diversions or can put himself to sleep; but he cannot avoid coming to himself now and then on waking up, at which time he immediately hears its awful voice. In his utmost depravity he can at most bring himself to the point where he no longer heeds it, but he cannot avoid hearing its voice.[98]

This apparently holds true, as Kant says, even for depraved men. But the moral man regards this voice in a special way; that is, his attitude toward the voice of conscience differs from the attitude of the depraved man. The moral man awakens to the voice, the depraved one attempts to silence it.[99] The moral man disciplines himself to be a good listener, and the discipline involved is one which Kant describes vividly.[100] The discipline of listening to and obeying the voice of conscience requires first that the hearer *presume* that the voice is not his own.[101] The hearer must presume that the voice of conscience originates *outside himself*. The reason for this is clear: if he recognized the voice—the accuser—as his own, then "the accuser would certainly lose every time."[102] What reason is there to obey or to fear or to stand in awe of my own voice? If I can make a rule, why can't I also break it? So to defeat the temptation to rationalize my own moral principles away, I must presume the voice is the voice of another.[103]

But that is still not enough! What if I were to imagine the voice to be that of my servant? I do not fear him anymore than I fear myself.[104]

---

[98] *Tugendlehre*, 7:250; Ellington, p. 101.

[99] *Tugendlehre*, 7:251n; Ellington, p. 101n.

[100] *Tugendlehre*, 7:251; Ellington, p. 101.

[101] Ibid.

[102] *Tugendlehre*, 7:250; Ellington, p. 100.

[103] *Tugendlehre*, 7:251; Ellington, p. 101.

[104] A servant does not possess authority over the one he serves.

It is necessary, Kant argues, to presume not only that the voice of conscience comes from another, but that the other be "a searcher of hearts"—one who cannot be fooled and one in front of whom one dare not lie.[105] As Kant says, this one is "all obligating," a moral being possessing "all authority (over heaven and earth), for otherwise he could not give proper effect to his laws."[106]

If this moral being is not thought of as God his voice could be easily silenced. As Kant puts it:

> a moral being possessing power over all is called *God*, so conscience must be conceived as the subjective principle of being accountable to God for one's deeds. Indeed, this concept of accountability is always contained (even if only in an obscure way) in every moral self-consciousness.[107]

Of course Kant is quick to point out that we therefore have no entitlement "to suppose that such a supreme being actually exists outside"[108] oneself. For that would clearly be trespassing into an intelligible world, violating one of the cardinal principles of critical philosophy.[109] We are not only permitted, we are obligated to presume that the voice of our conscience is the voice of God. This is to insure that the voice is *listened to* and *obeyed* each time it speaks.

So the discipline of morality consists, in part, of reinforcing the voice of conscience by construing its commands—originating really in reason[110]—as the commands of the Deity. The control, therefore, over the relationship between me and my conscience is a rationally self-constructed ideal designed by me to defeat my own natural tendencies to overlook my duties and to dismiss judgments unfavorable to my inclinations. This voice is, after all, the voice of a *judge*. In Kant's

---

[105]*Tugendlehre*, 7:251; Ellington, p. 101. Here the German for a "searcher of hearts" is "Herzenkündiger," literally a seer-into or a knower-of-hearts. This is a term out of German pietism.

[106]*Tugendlehre,* 7:252; Ellington, p. 102.

[107]Ibid.

[108]Ibid.

[109]Cf. "The Dialectic of Pure Reason," *Kl.*

[110]Cf. *Grundlegung*, 4, passim; Beck, passim.

account of conscience as an inner judge, a "searcher of hearts,"[111] he characterizes conscience as a shadow from which a person cannot run away.

The Typic of Practical Reason

In the *Critique of Practical Reason* there is a small section at the end of chapter 2, "Of the Typic of Pure Practical Judgment."[112] Here Kant reiterates many of the issues about judgment raised in the first *Critique.* The difference, though, is that Kant here makes explicit the fact that there can be no *schematism* for moral judgment. What connects the moral laws to nature is not a schema, because moral laws are not categories. What is applied to the world of sense is a "law of freedom," and the concept of the "absolutely good." The morally good, according to Kant, is a "supersensuous ideal."[113] There is, therefore, "nothing corresponding to it . . . in sensuous intuition."[114] It follows, according to Kant, that "no schema can be supplied for the purpose of applying it *in concreto.*"[115] Since no schema can be supplied, the understanding then creates for the purposes of judgment a "type" of the moral law for the "estimation of maxims according to moral principles":[116] in moral judgment, therefore, a "type" of the moral law takes the place of a schema. This is a difficult doctrine.

A "type" according to Kant, functions as a sort of symbol constructed out of aspects of the sensuous world. This symbol is "the type of an intelligible nature, so long as we do not carry over to the latter intuitions and what depends on them but only to apply to it the form of lawfulness in general."[117] We know, Kant says, that everything in nature proceeds according to laws. But we do not know anything

---

[111]*Tungendlehre*, 7:252; Ellington, p. 102.

[112]*KPR*, 5:75-79; Beck, pp. 70-74.

[113]*KPR*, 5:75; Beck, p. 70.

[114]*KPR*, 5:76; Beck, p. 71: *"sinnlichen Anschauung."*

[115]*KPR*, 5:77; Beck, p. 71.

[116]*KPR*, 5:78; Beck, p. 72.

[117]Ibid.

about supernature—so we commonly make use of a model of natural law as a "type" of the laws of supernature. In our common moral judgments we make use of a principle based upon this model.

> Ask yourself whether, if the action which you propose should take place by a law of nature of which you yourself were a part, you could regard it as possible through your will. Everyone does, in fact, decide by this rule whether actions are morally good or bad.[118]

This is, of course, the categorical imperative which, according to Kant, serves "only as a type of a law of freedom" for use in judging the morality of actions.[119] This process of estimation involving the "typic" of judgment is a process whose purpose is to guard against the use of practical reason in two damaging ways. Kant is concerned to show in the typic of judgment that there are two errors into which judgment can fall without the proper guidance from the typic of moral laws: the first is called the "empiricism of practical reason," the second is called the "mysticism of practical reason."[120] The former is the error basing "the practical concepts of good and evil on merely empirical consequences," and the latter is the error of making "into a schema that which should serve only as a symbol."[121] A person making the first error is guilty of using "empirical consequences" as the basis upon which moral principles are to rest. His moral principles are naturalistic. A person making the second error is guilty of "proposing

---

[118]Ibid.

[119]Kant's term for "judgment" in this context is "*Beurteilung.*" This term means to "estimate," "criticize," "review," or "judge." Its most ordinary usage is similar to our use of "judgment" in sentences like the following: "The umpire made a judgment call at first base. Though the replay of the throw shows that the runner tied the fielder, the umpire gave the call to the fielder. He wasn't in a position to see the play develop." The point here is an important one. When judgments are made, the judge has to make a decision (an estimation) based upon the facts he has at his disposal, facts which do not fully determine the case at hand. Moral judgments are often such decisions—they, too, are "judgment calls."

[120]*KPR,* 5:78; Beck, p. 73.

[121]Ibid.

to supply real yet nonsensuous intuitions (of an invisible Kingdom of God) for the application of the moral law."[122] The empiricist morality becomes a skepticism, while the mystical morality becomes dogmatic. The former bases its moral principles on *too little*, the latter bases its moral principles on *too much*.

Here it is argued that, based on Kant's account of the typic of judgment, the application of the categorical imperative requires a wisdom which is largely cautionary. A cautionary discipline must be erected to ensure against the improper construction of "typics". The typic is the expression of the moral law sketched out of materials taken from experience. It is, therefore, an example drawn from experience, only the form of which is applicable for the purposes of judging the morality of actions. A discipline is needed here to ensure first that the empirical elements of the example not be mistaken to be its formal content, and secondly that its elements are not imagined to be intuitions of a supersensuous reality.

The point Kant is making in the important section of the second *Critique* just mentioned is a difficult one to make clearly. He probably is saying that since the application to actual experience of moral rules requires an example for visualizing the formal requirements of the moral law, it is probably crucial that the example not be mistaken for anything else. Kant is quite explicit about two misusages: an empirical misuse and a mystical misuse. Both of these misuses can lead to the destruction of morality, but it is a difficult matter to understand how this is so. Kant's examples in this section are not clearly drawn.

Consider the following. Suppose that I am in a position to improve my financial situation by making a false promise. What I must guard against, Kant seems to be saying, is the tendency to construct an example of the moral law in such a way that it favors my own inclinations to make a profit. My example would include certain empirical facts that would favor my interests. Kant is explicit about this much:

> Now everyone knows very well that if he secretly permits himself to deceive, it does not follow that everyone else will do so, or that if, unnoticed by others, he is lacking in

---

[122]Ibid.

compassion, it does not mean that everyone else will immediately take the same attitude toward him.[123]

This is, it seems clear, a "typic," but a faulty one just because it contains as a part of its formulation a piece of empirical data (If I lie, it is true that not everyone else will) that gives an advantage to my inclinations. Thus the typic above is drawn too closely to the pattern of the way things actually are in the world rather than to the way they ought to be.

The need for caution arises then where there is a tendency to construct "typics" which have no prescriptive force since they too closely mirror practices regarded as "natural." I must discipline myself, then, to construct examples more favorable to the moral law than to the inclinations arising to defeat it.[124] The tendency to fail here is what Kant calls the "empiricism of practical reason." It is an attitude or way of thinking against which I must be vigilant, for that attitude "uproots the morality of intentions."[125] The empiricism of practical reason "substitutes for duty something entirely different, namely, an empirical interest, with which inclinations generally are secretly in league."[126]

This seems to be familiar Kantian territory. However, the discussions of the mysticism of practical reason are probably not. Kant recognizes that the threat to morality from mysticism is less urgent than the threat from empiricism because it is less frequently encountered. Mysticism, unlike empiricism, is not an ordinary way of thinking. Empirical attitudes are common; mystical attitudes are not. The mystic is guilty of "making into a schema that which should serve only as a symbol."[127] The mystic plunges into the transcendent, while

---

[123]KPR, 5:77; Beck, p. 72.

[124]For an illuminating discussion of all of the themes struggled with here see A. C. Genova's "Kant's Complex Problem of Reflective Judgment," The Review of Metaphysics 23 (1969-1970) 452-80. Genova's article contains a detailed account of reflective judgment, contrasting it with theoretical and moral judgments. Cf. pp. 463-65.

[125]KPR, 5:79; Beck, p. 74.

[126]Ibid.

[127]KPR, 5:78; Beck, p. 73.

the empiricist "yields to the currents of nature."[128] This plunge is a difficult one to describe.

We know that the mystic turns symbols into schema. What does that mean in practice? Abstractly it means that the mystic claims to construct his "typic" from supersensuous intuitions. His examples are constructed by "stretching his imagination" beyond the world of sense.[129] Kant suggests that the mystic "proposes to supply real yet nonsensuous intuitions (of an invisible Kingdom of God)."[130]

It is only with the help of some of Kant's later writings that the problem with mysticism and morality can be cleared up. Mystics, as Kant describes them in *Religion*, suppose that since they have been let in to peek at the inner workings of the "invisible kingdom," they are entitled to special dispensations in the visible world. Consequently they feel no longer bound by the moral law because they have looked upon its very source and have become "God's favorites."[131] A favorite in the house of God does not have to bother about being a servant. He does not have to obey the rules governing mere mortals. His works, he believes, neither add to nor subtract from a relationship with the Father that he has established in the first place by violating the rules of the game.[132]

While others, *mere servants* in God's Kingdom, do their duties and suffer what they must, mystics free themselves from these "tedious" chores, saying to those left behind: "As the Father was saying to me just the other day, 'Chores are there only for those not enthusiastic enough to address me in person'."[133] The *fanatics*, as Kant calls them, can usually be found among "a clergy having dominion over men's hearts." This dominion, Kant says, is achieved by the usurpation of

---

[128]Cf. the discussion of Hume in chapter one.

[129]*KPR*, 5:79; Beck, p. 74: *"seine Einbildungskraft bus übersinnlichen Anschauung anzuspannen."*

[130]*KPR*, 5:78; Beck, p. 73: *"eines unsichtbaren Reichs Gottes."*

[131]*Religion*, 6:352; Greene, p. 188.

[132]*Religion*, 6:352-53; Greene, pp. 188-90.

[133]Ibid.

"the prestige attached to exclusive possession of means of grace."[134] In the same section of *Religion* Kant gives his readers a graphic description of the mystical fanatic:

> The persuasion that we can distinguish the effects of grace from those of nature (virtue) or can actually produce the former within ourselves, is *fanaticism*; for we cannot, by any token, recognize a supersensible object in experience, still less can we exert an influence upon it to draw it down to us.[135]

The mystic is, according to Kant, one who mistakes the effects of the moral law for the effects of a supernatural power. He believes that the subjective constraints of the law are the "inner revelations" of "heavenly influences."[136] This attitude is, Kant says, "a kind of madness."[137] Even if it were true that our "supposed inner revelations" were born of heavenly influences, according to Kant, we could not distinguish them from others whose origins were merely rational. The mystic, as Kant puts it in the second *Critique* (here Kant is discussing the "extravagancies of genius"), squanders real treasures by promising visionary ones.[138]

The mistake of the mystic is a special one, requiring a distinct discipline. The "typic" constructed by the mystic is drawn closely enough to the pattern of the moral law, but it is mistaken to be what it is not: namely a revelation. His action would probably appear to be motivated by *too much* conviction, and he would appear to us as a *dogmatic* who is unreflective and un-self-critical. He would probably want to claim that his actions were willed not by himself but by God. This would damage morality simply because such action is not autonomous. Mysticism is, thus, a sort of supernatural heteronomy,

---

[134]*Religion*, 6:351; Greene, p. 188.

[135]*Religion*, 6:324; Greene, p. 162.

[136]Ibid.: "*Himmlische Einflüsse.*"

[137]Ibid.: "*ist eine Art Wahnsinn.*"

[138]*KPR*, 5:176; Beck, p. 167.

which robs action of that which makes it distinctively moral, namely, its rationally self-determining aspects.[139]

The Third *Critique* Doctrine of Judgment

The doctrine of judgment presented in the third *Critique* confirms, in a sense, the problem Kant was having in the previous two. The problem, as stated earlier, was that of judging in the absence of schemata. The first *Critique* notion of the subsumptioń of particulars under universal rules appeared again in the second *Critique* where it was argued that though in moral cases the particular is to be brought under rules—the rules of reason (laws of freedom) rather than the concepts or categories of the understanding—it is a mistake to expect schemata to perform the necessary subsumption. Kant there introduces the difficult notion of the typic. The typic was to be considered as the product of the imagination embodying the form of moral law in an example or maxim whose material is an image drawn after an empirical object or event. The general outlines of the first *Critique* doctrine of judgment remain intact; thus, in the second *Critique*, judgment is still described as an act of subsumption, but a subsumption proceeding in accordance with the operations of the imagination rather than the operations of the schematism. The strictures regulating the construction of typics, it has been argued, are aspects of a larger activity Kant called *discipline*.[140]

Discipline was said to consist of an array of subjective hindrances generated by the recognition of the moral law. These hindrances were identified as moral feelings or pure feelings, feelings having as their causes the actions of reason itself. The notion of reason-caused feelings, introduced in several places in Kant's works prior to the publication of the third *Critique*, is developed systematically in *The Critique of Judgment*.[141] *The Critique of Judgment* is really a critique of what Kant calls "the feeling of pleasure and displeasure."[142] It is a

---

[139]Ibid.

[140]Cf. sections 5 and 6 of this chapter.

[141]*K3*, passim; Meredith, passim.

[142]*K3*, 5:245; Meredith, pp. 15-16.

Critique designed to bridge the gap between nature and the laws of freedom, or rather a critique of the feelings which bridge the gap.[143]

According to Kant there are two classes of experiences in response to which some peculiar feelings arise.[144] When we are confronted either with objects the reflection on which reveals to us a "formal finality," or something "transcending all bounds of sense," there are awakened in us the feelings of the beautiful and the sublime.[145] The former, according to Kant, can be taken as a symbol (only a symbol) of the good, the latter as a token of the infinite extent to which *personality* transcends all standards of sense.[146] Of course this does not constitute the entire content of Kant's treatment of beauty and sublimity; it constitutes only that part of his treatment especially relevant to his moral philosophy.[147] What is abundantly clear is that Kant's moral philosophy appears explicitly throughout both parts of the third *Critique* and indeed constitutes the entire final one-quarter of the book.[148] The point is simply that the relevance of the third *Critique* to the moral philosophy cannot really be debated.[149] What needs to be

---

[143]In a section entitled "The Dwelling-Place of Judgment," A. C. Genova ("Kant's Complex Problems") argues that though the second *Critique* established a "contact" between nature and freedom, the third *Critique* develops a kind of "continuity" between them referred to in Kant's work as a "harmony" between sensible and the supersensible worlds. The gap between theory and practice, between the "ought" and the "is," is narrowed in the third *Critique* by the notion of reflective judgment.

[144]What is "peculiar" about them is that their origin is a priori.

[145]Cf. Meredith's "Analytical Index to Aesthetic Judgment" (in his translation of *K3*) for a list of where Kant uses these terms throughout *K3*, pp. 228-46.

[146]*K3*, 5, paragraph 27, passim; Meredith, "Analytical Index," pp. 105-109.

[147]Kant's entire treatment of the sublime is couched in a moral vocabulary. A cursory glance at the "analytic of the sublime" will make this quite clear.

[148]*K3*, 5:514-68; Meredith, pp. 98-163.

[149]Nahm, " 'Sublimity' and the 'Moral Law' " (chapter one), writes: "I shall argue that the conjunction of sublimity and moral law here as elsewhere

discussed is the precise connection between this last *Critique* and Kant's moral philosophy.

The *Critique of Judgment* consists of two lengthy introductions, a critique of aesthetic judgment, a critique of teleological judgment (including a section on the method of applying teleological judgment) and, finally, an appendix containing a moral proof of the existence of God.[150] The structure of the third *Critique* is complex. But however complex it may seem to the casual reader, it clearly has an elliptical structure with two focal points.[151] The first focus is the one which seems to have given Kant the most trouble and is accorded two separate introductions, only the last of which remains with the body of the work.[152] This first focus is the refashioned doctrine of judgment.

This new doctrine retains some of the features of the first and second *Critique* notions of judgment. I shall detail these differences later on in this section of my essay. The second focus must be mentioned, though, at this point.[153] It is to be found in the final sections of the *Critique* where it appears as a rich account of an ethico-theology, based upon a moral proof of the existence of God followed by an account of moral or practical faith.[154] This focus is clearly Kant's moral philosophy and not simply an account of the power of judgment. What is intended to be drawn from this important section of

---

in Kant's writings is important for an understanding of his ethics." The sublime, Nahm goes on to argue, is hardly aesthetic at all. It is almost entirely a moral concept in Kant's philosophy. With Nahm's judgment I am in full accord. Cf. pp. 502-503 of his article.

[150]See note 148 above for a reference to this part of *K3*.

[151]What is meant here is that though the work is unified, it is unified around two questions: What is judgment? and What is the relevance of the notion of purposiveness to morality?

[152]The "First Introduction" is, in English, now published separately by Bobbs-Merrill in the Library of Liberal Arts series of books (see the Bibliography).

[153]For a detailed account of the structure of *K3* see H. W. Cassirer's *A Commentary on Kant's Critique of Judgment* (New York: Barnes and Noble, Inc., 1938, 1970).

[154]Cf. also "Opining, Knowing, and Believing," *K1*, A820-30; B848-58.

the third *Critique* are the materials out of which to begin an account of Kant's notion of moral life, which shall then be developed carefully in chapter four of this essay.[155]

It is important at this point, however, to return to the matter of the relationship between the doctrine of judgment as it appears in the third *Critique* and the earlier treatment of it in the first two *Critiques*. It must be said that the significant difference between the notion of judgment in the third *Critique* and the previous two is a startling one. For though the notion of subsumption is retained this operation proceeds in a sort of cognitive vacuum.[156] Whereas the first and second *Critiques* both ruled out the schematism in judgments of the self-conscious kind, leaving a vacuum to be filled in by the disciplined spontaneity of law, the third *Critique* presents an additional and not quite parallel void.[157] Judgment, as it is finally presented in the third *Critique*, consists of the *rational construction of a universal* after the pattern of a form found in an isolated particular under which form the particular is then subsumed.[158] What is given is only the particular, which then has to serve as the foundation on which the universal has to be created.

This curious activity comes to represent, for Kant, the *disciplined spontaneity of reason*.[159] Here in the third *Critique* is a discussion of reason generating its own rules. This is important for an understanding of moral judgment because the central problem in Kant's moral philosophy is the question of how autonomous moral action is possible.[160]

---

[155]Cf. section 4 of this chapter.

[156]The universal is absent and must, therefore, be constructed.

[157]H. W. Cassirer in *A Commentary*, p. 116, puts it as follows: "Reflective judgment . . . . is interested in the relation of empirical laws and empirical concepts, but there are no universal objective concepts given to reflective judgment."

[158]What was at first novel, Kant says, becomes the rule.

[159]Cf. the discussion of pedantry above.

[160]The *typic* is as much imaginative as is a *symbol*: we must exercise "judgment" in the common sense of that term when we make moral decisions.

In the third *Critique* Kant contrasts what he calls "determinant" with "reflective" judgments.[161] Determinant judgments consist of the subsumption of particulars under already established universals. The concept under which particulars are to be subsumed is already *defined*, and the activity of judging consists of determining whether a given object "fits" under it. Thus, determinant judgments determine whether or not a particular falls under a defined universal. The product of such judgments is what Kant calls "knowledge."

Reflective judgments differ from determinant ones in that (a) no defined universals are available for the subsumption of particulars, (b) the particulars are considered qua particular, and (c) a universal is constructed after the pattern of a form contained in the particular itself. The universal, instead of preceding the particular, is generated by a *reflection on it*.[162] Kant's models of reflective judgments come from two different areas: the estimate of works of art (judgments of taste) and the estimation of the purposiveness of organisms (judgments of purpose).[163]

The judgment that a work of art is beautiful is not an objective (determinant) judgment. Judgments of taste are subjective in the sense that they are statements about the feeling of the harmony of certain sensations with the rules of unity of the understanding.[164] The designedness of works of art produces pleasures in the subject disinterestedly attentive to them. Judgments of taste are judgments about the manifold of feeling.

Similarly, we judge of the purposiveness of organisms by constructing concepts in accordance with which organisms could have

---

This indicates that we must decide which aspects of situations are relevant to particular moral rules, a decision procedure which is certainly not *algorithmic*. Our decisions are, to that extent, autonomous.

[161]Cf. *K3*, paragraph 75.

[162]A. C. Genova, "Kant's Complex Problem," p. 457, writes: "To reflect is to turn over in one's mind, to compare and coordinate one's thoughts so as to find a rule or law that fits an otherwise unintelligible situation and makes sense of it."

[163]These two are related to each other in the introductions to *K3*.

[164]*K3*, 5:254; Meredith, p. 28.

been *designed* or *created* and which appear to serve ends of their own as well as other ends of nature.[165] Yet these concepts are reflective constructions which do not yield knowledge of organisms. Instead they integrate otherwise inchoate experiences into a rational ideal of a nature whose creator is not simply a *first cause* (a Deity), but an *Author* of nature.[166]

Reflective judgments organize, therefore, not a manifold of intuition or a manifold of desire, but a manifold of feeling. It can be said that we *know* nature discursively, we *typify* moral rules, and we *suspect* purposiveness.[167]

The connection between the second and third *Critiques* can now be established. Reflective judgments are expressions of our *suspicions* that the moral and the natural realms are unified in the supersensible.[168] Since such unity cannot be known it is symbolized in our works of art and in our experiences of natural beauty and the purposiveness of organisms.[169]

What this means for morality is quite clear. Since our actions *typify* moral laws (they are commanded) they would soon become perfunctory could they not be suspected to harmonize with some larger, yet unknown supersensible unity.[170] The actions in our lives must, at least, be felt to add up to something in the context of a larger system beyond our experience. Aesthetic experience provides us with symbols of that larger system, the reflection on which provides a

---

[165]*K3*, 5:444-47; Meredith, pp. 12-16.

[166]*K3*, 5:534; Meredith, p. 121.

[167]A. C. Genova, "Kant's Complex Problem," p. 478, writes: "We *know* nature, we *think* the purposes of reason, but in aesthetic experience, we *feel* purposiveness."

[168]Since we cannot *know* about any actual harmony between the natural and moral worlds, the aesthetic construction (the reflective consideration) of such harmony produces feelings similar to the feeling of the beautiful and the sublime.

[169]Similarly, the designedness of works of art and the purposiveness of organisms cannot be *known*; they can be *felt*.

[170]The point here is that there is a felt harmony between what might be called the micro-moral and the macro-moral.

context in which the typification of moral principles becomes purposeful.[171] The aesthetic aspect of moral experience is therefore its *religious dimension*.

The connection, then, between the third *Critique* doctrine of judgment and Kant's moral philosophy is this: reflective judgments about the unity of the moral and the natural world (the two standpoints of the *Groundwork*) create a systematic context in which moral actions can be felt to be purposeful. The idea of purposefulness serves as an incentive added to those already said to be contained a priori in the recognition of duties. So, although Kant's *moral theory* is deontological (acts are commanded absolutely, regardless of punishments or rewards), it is given *in practice* an aesthetic dimension which is the reflective construction of the agent himself. In this reflectively constructed cosmos the agent's actions are seen in a context which gives them meaning—a meaning which can be said to consist of the harmony of his *life* with what Kant had earlier called the Kingdom of Ends.

Kant, of course, recognized that morality might (and often does) collapse if the agent were not able to convince himself of the ultimate harmony of the natural and the moral worlds. Since this harmony could not possibly be known, it must, therefore, be *thought* and it is something about which a moral agent must become convinced. Otherwise his attempts to act morally would be swallowed up in a blind mechanism of nature. The construction of a cosmos which rewards virtue and punishes evil, which provides a reflective ground for hope, is both an aesthestic act and the sine qua non of religiousness.

It is possible to see that there is an analogy between Kant's notion of reflective judgment and the notion of moral discipline. Just as a scientist must construct a hypothetical nature in which organisms are purposive so that he may be provided with guiding threads for further investigations, the person faced with a moral decision—faced with having to make a moral judgment—must also construct a hypothetical context in which his actions will have meaning. The construction of both hypothetical natures and hypothetical moral worlds (ectypal

---

[171]Another way to put it is to say that *tactics* make sense only within the context of *strategy*.

worlds) requires a carefully managed thinking process—a creative process which, nevertheless, is rule-guided. Both reflective judgments and moral judgments, when not carefully constrained by discipline, fail by being either too idealistic or too narrow. The point is that the thinking process which leads to reflective or to moral judgments can go wrong by being too responsive to abstract ideals, or too responsive to present realities. Moral and reflective judgments must be carried on in an intellectual atmosphere which is equally affected by idealities and actual contingencies.

There is only one discipline of reason. Theoretical, moral, and artistic activities are all equally constrained by reason's one discipline. Reason's discipline prevents the theoretician from getting lost in antinomy, the moral agent from being fanatical or skeptical, and the artist from both egocentric fantasy and an unfocused diffuseness. Thought *generally* fails in each of the three separate ways mentioned above—in the mysticisms, empiricisms, and pedantries of reason. Reason's discipline is corrective of these regardless of the content of thought. Discipline would not be necessary were thought itself purely mechanical procedure. Since it is creative and spontaneous, as Kant says, it must be *guided*, rather than *compelled*, by carefully maintained intellectual and emotional postures.[172]

Summary

A few of the aspects of Kantian moral philosophy have now been introduced which lend credence to the notion that moral judgment is not really a calculus, but is instead a discipline of sorts. The idea of a moral discipline is an attractive one. For if we imagine morality to consist, as Kant does, of a special attitude toward ourselves and others, or even as a particularly arduous way of seeing and thinking about things, it is clear that its discipline must consist of certain efforts designed to prevent the collapse of that attitude.

In nearly all of Kant's moral writings there is evidence of the struggle—the labor—required for the maintenance of moral attitudes. His doctrine is that moral attitudes are maintained by a discipline that is the product of the clear apprehension of moral principles. The

---

[172]See chapter five.

incentives generated by rational norms are felt as they suppress attitudes which compete with the moral one. The mistakes in moral practice are usually attributable to a collapse of moral attitudes caused by improper apprehension of moral principles. Moral living ceases, we might say, when we are convinced either too little or too much by rational norms.

The empiricist, failing to find an impossible certainty in his own rational norms, ceases to believe in them altogether and is therefore released from them to flounder in the currents of nature. He is incapable of convictions which would pressure him to improve his conduct. The distance between his norms and his practice disappears altogether. Kant's pictures of him reveal something more than a wayward epistemologist. He is rather an anti-intellectual of the most pernicious sort, whose own life illustrates his lack of conviction.

On the other hand, the mystic, believing that his rational norms are messages from the Deity, is convinced of too much. He is both impetuous and dogmatic. He is a fanatic. His life can be pictured as an especially bumpy one. He is the true enthusiast, whose activities seem to be unchecked by discipline or intelligence.

While the empiricist is too far away from norms that would steady his course, the mystic is too close and goes overboard in a "plunge" that shows him to be a fool. Both of these men live out of attitudes which are improperly disciplined. The former is unimaginative, the latter is too imaginative. But what about the pedant? Where does he fit into this taxonomy of characters?

The pedant, as Kant sees him, was introduced to illustrate an attitude equally as destructive of morality as the other two. Pedantry is a very special attitude. Kant calls it obtuseness and narrow-mindedness. The pedant recognizes moral norms, but manages to spirit away their powers by viewing them too narrowly. He is, therefore, overconcerned about all of the details of procedure, a fact that makes of him a priggish sort of character. He is so over-serious, we might suggest, that he is unable to be intelligently selective in his interpretations of the norms he recognizes. Life thus passes him by while he is busy making some new and more subtle and useless distinction.

We can say of the pedant that his moral attitudes are too carefully managed. He is too careful, but he is not a skeptic. His moral paralysis is a result not of lack of conviction but of his reluctance to make any concessions to inexactitude or to take any risks that might well turn out to have been fruitful. Another way to put it is to say that he is mechanical. Morality for him must always be an acute and paralyzing form of hyper-self-consciousness, preventing him from taking advantage of the spontaneity of the laws he so carefully inspects.

Moral discipline is Kant's answer to the problems we have with these attitudes. Moral discipline consists of the practice of managing moral attitudes and suppressing, as necessary, all the others that naturally compete with morality.[173]

In the next chapter will be presented an enlarged picture of the life of the moral man from its beginning to its end.[174]

---

[173]What this comes to mean is that discipline consists of the efforts required to construct rational macro-moral systems. See section 4, chapter 5.

[174]See chapter four.

Chapter Four

Kant
on the Revolution
of Perspectives

The Kantian distinction between acting in accord with duty and acting for the sake of duty, the former characterizing the legality and the latter the morality of actions, announces ultimately that moral worth is a function not of the conduct of persons, but of the distinctively moral "cast of mind," the virtue of the persons to whom the conduct is imputed.[1] Kant, like his predecessor Plato, believed that there is a profound difference between the naive man whose actions are

---

[1] *K3*, 5:237; Meredith, p. 104. Meredith translates *"die Gemütsstimmung"* here as both "cast of mind" and "temper of mind." Kant is literally talking about the quality or disposition of a person under the influence of the moral law. Kant's use of *"Gemütsstimmung"* in this context makes it clear that for him morality is a "frame of mind," a "mood," etc. What is interesting about this third *Critique* section (paragraphs 27-29) is that he identifies morality with a mood or feeling-tone produced by the consciousness of the moral law.

right but nevertheless based only upon "right opinion," and the reflective man whose actions are right because they are properly related to, and flowing from, principles correctly apprehended. Moral life, for Kant, consists of more than the conformance of conduct to objective moral principles. Morality is then less a matter of conduct than it is a matter of the progressive perfection of the springs of action—the progressive expression in conduct of a good will.

In the *Groundwork* Kant is concerned with showing that in spite of the countless efforts of various philosophers to deny the reality of "this disposition," as a "phantom of the imagination," it is nevertheless the birthright of each rational being.[2] That each possesses it is evident first in the fact that each admires and even respects those persons in whose conduct it seems manifest, and secondly in the fact that each, when confronted with an example of a violation of the moral law, is able, prior to any strenuous philosophizing, to recognize the violation, even if unable to articulate the grounds upon which his judgment had been made. This testifies to the fact that common human reason contains a law whose recognition provides the incentives necessary in themselves for moral living. But the mere possession of the seeds of morality in one's own common human reason cannot, and does not, guarantee its possessor a moral life.

This is to say that *in practice*, rather than in theory, morality is an inner disposition—what Kant had meant by the *good will* all along.

[2]I am here connecting two passages in *Grundlegung*, 263-64; Beck, p. 23. Kant's word for "disposition" is *"Gesinnung."* Kant writes: *"Daher es zu aller Zeit Philosophen gegeben hat, welche die Wirklichkeit dieser Gesinnung in den menschlichen Handlungen schlechterdings abgeleugnet, und alles der mehr oder weniger verfeinerten Selbstliebe zugeschrieben haben,"* and *"Mann kann auch denen, die Sittlichkeit als blosses Hirngespinst einer durch Eigendünkel sich selbst übersteigen menschlichen Einbildung verlachen"* (4:263-64). Some philosophers have denied, therefore, that morality as a disposition, a way of thinking, and attitude, exists. Kant argues throughout his works that they are wrong. Empiricists have denied, Kant argues, (1) that moral laws are a priori, (2) that the recognition of laws can produce incentives to action, and (3) that, therefore, morality is primarily dispositional. Kant argues that to concede to them any of the above a sure triumph for them is guaranteed. If they triumph genuine morality is cast aside. The empiricists are here accused of being too lazy to distinguish a priori principles from empirical generalizations, and also from creatures of pure fancy.

Plato's doubts about men who act on the basis of right opinion alone (instinctively, we might say) are shared by Kant for reasons quite similar to Plato's. The naive man, since he has no love for knowledge, cannot anchor his actions or his beliefs in anything permanent. What this means for Plato is clear. The naive man can be talked out of his beliefs by sophists. He is therefore at the mercy of the tides of public opinion, ultimately does damage to his own soul, and can look forward (according to the myth of Er) to a future life of tyranny.[3]

Similarly, Kant believes that the man of good nature acting instinctively (or because of external coercion) is condemned to a life oscillating feverishly between two amoral extremes. He is both fascinated and repelled by each of the two powers competing for his attention. Since he has not "taken the step into philosophy" he never manages to purify the springs of his own conscience, and he can either be talked out of what he knows dimly to be right, or he can too easily represent to himself the callings of the inclinations in the guise of morality. The natural man is always, therefore, in the position of being able to pervert his own good will by lying to himself. His life, like that of Plato's man of correct opinion, is, if good, the result of good fortune rather than of good will. The luxury of fortunate circumstances is to be credited with what goodness there is in his life, while he is to be blamed himself for the failure to free himself from the chains of natural habit, chains which may (and often do) lead him from the path of goodness.

It can be said that men of good nature live, according to Kant, lives quite similar to those of the prisoners inhabiting Plato's cave. And it can be said as well that the problem confronting each of them—the problem of how to free themselves—is addressed by Kant in a way quite similar to that of Plato.

It is intended in this chapter to discuss the life of the man who is moral in Kant's sense of the term. The next chapter will present a sketch of the life of the Kantian moral man, based primarily upon four of Kant's later essays: *The Conjectural Beginnings of Human History; Idea for a Universal History from a Cosmopolitan Point of View; The Failure of All Attempted Philosophical Theodicies;* and *The End of All Things.*[4]

---

[3]Plato, *Republic*, 10.614b—10.621d.

[4]*Mutmasslicher Anfang der Menschengeschichte (1786),* 4, hereafter

These essays provide the material necessary for the student of Kant to construct, as is done in chapter five, an ideal moral biography, to see what special problems might face a person attempting to live a moral life as Kant pictures it.[5]

---

cited as *Beginnings; Idee zu einer allgemeinen Geschichte in weltbügerlicher Absicht* (1784), 4, hereafter cited as *Idea; Theodicee;* and, *Das Ende aller Dinge* (1794), 6, hereafter cited as *Ende.* Translations cited as follows: *Theodicee*, by Michel Despland, appearing as an appendix to his *Kant on History and Religion;* the translations of the other three essays appear in Lewis White Beck's collection of Kant's historical writing, *On History.*

[5]The notion of "radical evil" is dealt with fully in chapters seven and eight of Despland, *Kant on History and Religion*, pp. 157-215. In a footnote (38, p. 328) Despland writes: "Evil lies in man's choice, not his constitution. It is a spiritual act, not a bodily determination. Fallen man's propensity to evil lies not in his physical nature but in his moral nature (which is 'an expression of freedom'), namely in the habits or dispositions resulting from the repeated use of evil maxims; it lies in 'the subjective ground of the exercise of man's freedom in general'." However, as with almost every other story in Kant, this plot thickens considerably. The "habits" that are built up by the "repeated use of evil maxims" are described in *Theodicee* as nearly impossible to extirpate, and thus become what Kant calls a sort of "second nature." Note that what is often called "original sin" is a "second nature." Adam and Eve became sinful by eating fruit from the forbidden tree. They were, in consequence, blown out of paradise and incapable of ever returning.

The difference between Kant's radical evil and original sin is not an impressive one, though it is often thought to be. Radical evil is radical just because it is so deeply woven into the fabric of human consciousness as a second nature. So is original sin. What is apparent is that radical evil, as it is pictured in Kant's work, is nearly impossible to extirpate. (I do not know how important the word "nearly" is in this context.) Thus the great paradox of Kantian morality (and of Protestantism generally): we are categorically commanded to extirpate that which is nearly ineradicable. It is no wonder that Kant is driven in *Religion* to say that after we have worked our hardest to extirpate radical evil we have a right to hope for supernatural assistance (grace). No other assistance would be much good. It is this paradox which haunts the Kantian moral philosophy with its *melancholia.* Cf. Walter Benjamin's *The Origin of German Tragic Drama* for a brilliant discussion of the paradox and of its resulting *melancholia.*

Commenting on the absence of developed concepts of love and sin, Iris Murdoch, *(The Sovereignty of Good* [New York: Schocken Books, 1971] pp. 46-47) says that contemporary ethical theories need to take these concepts

Summary of Previous Three Chapters

Chapters one and two introduced Kant's notion of common human reason in order to focus upon the efforts required to locate and to isolate the moral law which it was said to contain. The object there was to emphasize the subjective aspects of Kant's formal moral theory. The law was shown there to have a subjective stabilizing influence upon the emotional life while at the same time being the carrier of objective moral principles. In chapter three was discussed the notion of judgment found in the three *Critiques* in order to show its connection to Kant's notion of discipline defined there as cautionary or negative wisdom. Discipline, it was argued, developed gradually as a corrective and a guide to moral judgment.

The importance of discipline cannot be overstated. For in the absence of a schematism to connect moral theory to moral practice, something both rational and creative is required which must be looked after carefully so that it does not land in either the empiricisms or mysticisms of practical reason. The discipline described in chapter two is clearly not a "faculty" that becomes active only at the moment of moral choice. Discipline erects a series of attitudes toward the world and the persons in it that continue "in between" specific moral choices.[6] In short, discipline creates a way of life, not just the exercise of some isolated talent or skill. The moral way of life is maintained as an attitude that pervades living first as an unusually unnatural and strained way of looking at the different experiences of life. Gradually it

---

more seriously. Murdoch cites Kierkegaard's "an ethic which ignores sin is an altogether useless science" but is careful to include the rest, i.e., "but if it recognizes sin it is *eo ipso* beyond its sphere." It is this sort of tension which animates Kantian moral philosophy as well.

[6]Iris Murdoch, *The Sovereignty of Good*: "The moral life, on this view, is something that goes on continually, not something that is switched off in between the occurrence of explicit moral choices." Similarly: "But if we consider what the work of attention is like, how continuously it goes on, and how imperceptibly it builds up structures of value round about us, we shall not be surprised that at crucial moments of choice most of the business of choosing is already over. But it implies that the exercise of our freedom is a small piecemeal business which goes on all the time and not a grandiose leaping about unimpeded at important moments" (p. 37).

becomes less strained, but it never can become a second nature, according to Kant. Morality can never become totally habitual.[7]

The reason for this should be clear. The essence, we might say, of morality is freedom. The moral person is never free of moral laws; he is free because of them. Should morality ever become habitual, the freedom which is its essence would vanish. Habitual morality is really a contradiction, except perhaps in a being with a holy will. But then it would no longer be called "morality" but "holiness" instead. Since morality cannot become habitual, it always requires of its practioners a disciplined pilgrimage of struggle. The end of struggle is also the end of morality.

Before presenting a sketch of an ideal Kantian moral biography— the life, that is, of the person whose attitudes are disciplined morally— a description shall be presented of the demands and the dimensions of the moral attitudes constituting the subjective aspect of Kantian moral theory. It should be clear from this description why Kant insists upon the non-habitual character of morality.

The Wire-Walker

Maintaining oneself in the moral attitude is a strenuous business, as Kant pictures it. It is strenuous because it represents really a sort of wire-walking, which, to begin with, is difficult to imagine and even moreso to accomplish. It requires constant maintenance. Just when one thinks one has mastered the moral perspective he falls off the wire one way or the other, or he simply stands still.

The empiricist, pictured earlier, simply gives up the effort to stay aloft, yields to the currents of nature, and falls off. The mystic, while imagining himself to be an adept, takes a plunge, because he is forever

---

[7]*Anthropologie*, 8:32-35; Gregor, pp. 26-29; "Virtue is, rather, *moral strength* in pursuing our duty, which never becomes habit but should always spring forth, quite new and original, from our way of thinking *(Denkungsart)*." And, *"habit (assuetudo)*, however, is a physical inner necessitation to continue behaving the same way we have behaved so far. It deprives even good actions of their moral value because it detracts from our freedom of mind; moreover, it leads to thoughtless repetition of the same action (mechanical uniformity) and so becomes ridiculous."

sure that his heaven-directed gaze will relieve him of the necessity to watch where he is going. The pedant, while perhaps examining either the creases in his shoes or the textures of the wire itself, remains in the same place and is therefore unable to take pleasure in his progress, for progress to him feels like falling. Each of these characters has failed to develop properly disciplined attitudes, and has consequently failed to master, in one way or the other, the attitudes competing with the moral one for supremacy. Though there may be no exhaustively determinable rules to guide a moral wire-walker, there are "guiding-threads."[8]

The wire-walking analogy being developed here needs to be clarified a bit before the notion of a guiding-thread can be placed in its proper perspective. The analogy here is based primarily upon the familiar *Groundwork* discussion of the two standpoints. The reader will recall the following passage:

> For this reason a rational being must regard himself as intelligence (and not from the side of his lower powers), as belonging to the world of understanding and not to that of the senses. Thus he has two standpoints from which he can consider himself and recognize the laws of the employment of his powers and consequently of all his actions: first, as belonging to the world of sense under laws of nature (heteronomy), and, second, as belonging to the intelligible world under laws which, independent of nature, are not empirical but founded only on reason.[9]

The wire-walker analogy is constructed as follows: the wire is suspended between the intelligible and the sensible worlds (above and below) and connected to platforms on each end representing, respectively, birth and death. A refusal to mount the wire constitutes, for Kant, an expression of the enslavement to nature and to her habits. Such a person remains in perpetual tutelage under nature's powerful

---

[8]Kant's word is *"Leitfaden."* Cf. *K3*, 5, paragraph 72; Meredith, p. 40: "A guiding-thread for the purpose of becoming acquainted with the character of these things by means of observation, without trenching upon an investigation into their first origin."

[9]*Grundlegung*, 4:312; Beck, p. 71.

laws. And, of course, walking the wire is here analogized to living a moral life elevated to such a point that it can be said to occupy two standpoints—that of nature and of reason. The metaphor of the wire is intended to convey the sense of the delicate balance needed to maintain oneself in both worlds at the same time. This balance is effected by virtue of the incentives (*Triebfedern*) generated by the recognition of rational principles apprehended in the standpoint directed toward the intelligible world, incentives which make possible the rational control of the inclinations which are generated in man by nature.

Rationality, for Kant, gives man two very different powers with which he is able to direct his passage from one end of the wire to the other. Rationality enables him, first, to be convinced of the efficacy of reason itself, and secondly to know nature as she appears to him. It is important to note here that being convinced of something is qualitatively different from knowing something.[10]

In the third *Critique* Kant describes the relationship of man to nature as the relationship of the judge to the witness.[11] Man questions nature with the conviction, founded on a rational faith, that nature will answer questions properly addressed. The point is this: the belief in the efficacy of rationality makes the knowledge and then the mastery of nature possible. To suppose that the order is reversed, to suppose, that is, that knowledge is necessary in order to provide grounds for conviction condemns us to a predicament similar to David Hume's. We will discover that knowledge is impossible, and we will then be forced into a skepticism from which convictions would be impossible. We would then find ourselves isolated from the sources of our humanity, and we would be unable even to conceive of a reason practical enough to make a moral life possible.

It is the conviction, therefore, in the efficacy of reason that makes the initial step onto the wire possible. Once that step has been taken the initial conviction is reinforced by the knowledge which it had made possible. The moral law provides moral amateurs with an array of

---

[10]Cf. *K1*, A828-31; B856-59, for Kant's discussion of the differences between *logical certainties* and *moral convictions*. Cf. *K3*, Paragraph 91.

[11]This questioning process is the primary topic of most of the "Critique of Teleological Judgment."

incentives which pull, push, and guide the walker on the wire. It is attractive (the more so the more clearly it is apprehended), it is goading, and it is direction-finding. But, since it can never be an object of direct experience, its effects on us are always dependent upon our own cooperation. It does not enslave our wills. It provides us, Kant says, with guiding-threads which we may either choose to follow out or not. Similarly, it humbles the pretensions we may have of being able to direct our courses without its aid. Its voice is gentle and firm.

Kant's notion of conscience—the notion of a voice which both humbles our pride and guides our progress—provides one of the links between moral theory and moral practice. It generates a series of subjectively felt hindrances here likened to the feelings a wire-walker might have just as he begins to lose his balance on the wire. These feelings (moral ones, of course) are dimmed or absent in the consciousness of one not attentive to the moral law. The more practiced we become in listening to the voice of conscience the more articulated it becomes and the finer are the detections of a loss of balance. The danger involved in guiding oneself by this voice is primarily that of not recognizing it as one's own voice—that is, of misinterpreting its messages. Our natural tendency, Kant suggests in several places, is for us to interpret what it says to us so as to do the least damage to our own interests. This tendency which is called "worthlessness" and "the inclination to lie to oneself," is, for Kant, the tendency against which the moral person must be vigilant.[12] A failure to apprehend the voice of conscience represents a total loss of the moral perspective. A loss of perspective is the most destructive of the moral way of life.

We are, therefore, free to live a moral life just to the extent that we are obedient to the voice of conscience. It is the voice and the feelings generated in us by our recognition of it that support our precarious position as beings inhabiting two different worlds. But before we can become attuned to the voice of conscience, we must first be able to hear it as something other than background noise. This requires, according to Kant, a Copernican revolution of attitudes. Quite literally, we must "turn around" in our own minds, as it were, to catch a first glimpse of

---

[12]*Theodicee*, 6:134-38; Despland, pp. 293-97.

conscience or to hear its faint murmurings. The issue is pretty clear at this point. One will not be able to walk the wire unless one has revolutionized his "cast of mind."[13] How this revolution occurs, according to Kant, furnishes the reader with a very interesting and difficult problem.

The Revolution of Attitude

In an early section of the *Anthropology* entitled, "On Voluntary Consciousness of Our Ideas," Kant says that becoming conscious of our ideas is really a matter either of "paying attention to" or "turning away from" them.[14] The former he calls "*attentio*," the latter "*abstractio*." Abstraction, he remarks, is not "merely neglecting to pay attention, failing to do it (that would be distraction, *distractio*); we are rather performing a real act of the cognitive power by which one idea of which we are conscious is held apart from its connections with other ideas in one consciousness."[15] Kant continues in an important passage to connect this power of consciousness to having one's own mind under control.

> The ability to abstract from an idea, even when the senses urge it on us, is a far greater power that that of paying attention to it; for it demonstrates a freedom of the power of judgment and the autonomy of the mind, by which the state of its ideas is under control (*animus sui compos*). In this respect the power of *abstraction*, when it deals with sense representations, is much more difficult to exercise than the power of attention, but also more important.[16]

To show why this is so—why, that is, abstraction is more difficult and more important than paying attention to ideas—Kant presents his readers with the following humorous example:

Many men are unfortunate because they cannot abstract.

---

[13] *K3*, 5:327; Meredith, p. 104; see also note 1 above.

[14] *Anthropologie*, 8:15-16; Gregor, p. 13.

[15] Ibid.

[16] Ibid.

The suitor could make a good marriage if only he could disregard a wart on his beloved's face or a missing tooth.[17]

The problem here is a familiar one. It is important, though, because of the principle it expresses. One must learn to exercise the freedom one has to abstract from the natural appearances of things in order to see them justly. This power of abstraction when fully operative represents the revolution in one's way of thinking necessary for moral living. A failure to use this power, or to exercise it well enough, condemns us to be at the mercy of the natural look of things, which also imprisons us in attitudes which are easy, natural, and morally impoverished.

The point is made clear in a passage from the same section of the *Anthropology*:

But our power of attention is guilty of particularly bad manners if it immediately fastens, even involuntarily, on others' shortcomings; to direct our eyes to a button missing from the coat of someone we are face to face with, or a gap between his teeth, or to fasten our attention on an habitual speech defect not only disconcerts him but also spoils our own chances of social success.[18]

The involuntariness of "bad manners" is a relaxation of our power of abstraction, a power clearly related to moral ways of seeing:

If a man is essentially good, it is not only fair, but also prudent, to *shut our eyes* to his misfortune and even to our own good fortune. But this power of abstracting is a strength of mind that we acquire only by practice.[19]

It is true that we acquire it only by practice; it is nevertheless the case that its initial acquisition is the result of a revolution that produces a reversal in our ordinary ways of thinking. The revolution destroys natural habits of thought so that moral thinking and seeing can replace them. The reversal of thinking, once accomplished, requires constant maintenance, and that maintenance is what Kant calls moral

---

[17]Ibid.

[18]Ibid.

[19]Ibid.

discipline. But we still have to explain how this revolution takes place, and how it can be known to have taken place either in ourselves or in others. The attempt to explain it, as will become evident shortly, is difficult philosophically, but also interesting.

Kant's metaphor of the revolution in a way of thinking seems to have been adopted from two different traditions. In Plato's *Republic*, one of the prisoners in the cave breaks the chains that bind him to his way of life, and then he turns around in his mind. *Strephein* is the term Plato uses for this turning. In the allegory Plato does not really give his readers many hints about what enabled this single prisoner to "free himself." One assumes, though, that a sort of dialectic or reflection is involved. What is clear, nevertheless, is that the *strephein* represents a turning away from the ordinary world of sense experience, toward the light coming from the sun.[20]

The other metaphor operating in Kant's account comes from the Judeo-Christian tradition. It is the metaphor of "repentance." The initial assumption of a moral way of thinking seems to be the result of some such act. Kant in the *Anthropology* remarks that a man finally gets sick and tired of the "precarious state of instinct" and in a single explosive act renounces his former way of life. Renunciation marks the beginnings of a moral life of freedom. One somehow notices that one is a slave to instinct, recognizes in the faint voice of conscience a call to freedom, and in the consciousness of a newly discovered power one renounces one's former way of life and at the same time resolves to live a new one. Initially, *repentance* and *strephein* are induced by the recognition of the painful state of acquiescing in the mores, customs and manners of non-reflective life. The two terms then suggest a turning away from that way of life.

Kant never tires of offering his readers rich illuminating descriptions of the impoverishment of the attitudes governing lives immersed thoughtlessly in the contingencies of politics. In Kant's last lengthy work, *The Strife of the Faculties* (1798),[21] written just six years before his death, he presents an account of the vagaries of ordinary life

---

[20]Cf. "Allegory of the Cave," Plato, *Republic*.

[21]*Der Streit der Fakultäten in drei Abschnitten* (1798), 7:395-96; Beck, *On History*, pp. 141-42.

and the attitudes engendered by that life. From the ordinary perspectives—common-sense realism and empiricism—of the man of the world, who views the history of the human race from the standpoint of common sense, the especially vulgar facets of human nature seem to dominate his point of view.

Kant's concern in a section of this work is to show that it is possible to *abstract* from the events and scandals which ordinarily catch one's attention in order to see a steady progress of the race from a state of savagery (the virtues of the pagans are but splendid vices) toward a cooperative republican world government under whose laws the predisposition to the good, as he calls it, can flourish. This over-looking of the seamy aspects of community life requires a strength of mind brought on by a Copernican revolution in thought. Without that revolution our visions are clouded:

> If the course of human affairs seems so senseless to us, perhaps it lies in a poor choice of position from which we regard it. Viewed from the earth, the planets sometimes move backwards, sometimes forward, and sometimes not at all. But if the standpoint selected is the Sun, an act which only reason can perform, according to the Copernican hypothesis they move constantly in their regular courses. Some people, however, who in other respects are not stupid, like to persist obstinately in their way of explaining the phenomena and in the point of view which they have once adopted, even if they should thereby entangle themselves to the point of absurdity in Tychonic cycles and epicycles.[22]

Thus, to see the course of human events as a steady progress, rather than a sequence of senseless absurdities, one must revolutionize one's perspective—a revolution which, Kant insists, requires an act of reason.

This act of reason—the revolution—involves the assumption of "the standpoint of Providence which is situated beyond all human wisdom."[23] The attempt to assume this stance requires that we do violence to our ordinary and natural way of seeing things. The

---

[22]Ibid.

[23]Ibid.

fundamental subjective difference between the two stances—the natural and the rational stances—is that the former is easy and costs us no effort, the latter requires a distinctively moral attitude involving a constant struggle. The former is the function of indolence, laziness, and intellectual servitude. The latter requires that we convince ourselves of the priority of rational ideals, gradually becoming embodied in the course of events by the free choices of moral men, and by the unseen workings of a beneficent Providence.

Kant's notion of Providence is a regulative idea. What this means has been the subject of some controversy. William A. Galston, for example, in his *Kant and the Problem of History* notes that

> there is in Kant's historical thought a sharp distinction between institutional and moral change. He holds out to us the possibility that institutional progress will lay the foundation for a sweeping moral reformation without really describing concretely the link between the former and the latter (indeed, while appearing to deny on theoretical grounds that any such link is possible).[24]

Galston fails to take Kant's notion of regulative ideas very seriously. Postulating a "link" is different from establishing one, yet Galston supposes Kant to have attempted the latter. Kant's notion of Providence is a regulative idea which serves not to *describe* the causes of human progress, but to provide incentives to reinforce moral motives in the life of the agent who is in danger of losing his perspective.

Again the problem is that without disciplined moral attitudes it is easy to take dim views of human affairs. This is true, according to Kant, in both politics and in ethics. Naturally we are suspicious of the intentions of others and of the competence of whatever is directing the course of human events. We must make serious efforts to suppress attitudes that cast "realistic" doubts upon the integrity of our moral ideals. Because without them—moral ideals—our lives and the lives of

---

[24]William A. Galston, *Kant and the Problem of History* (Chicago: University of Chicago Press, 1975) pp. 70-71, 73-74, 90-93, 269-70. Cf. *Idea*, 4:153-56; Beck, pp. 13-16.

our communities begin to degenerate into what Kant calls "luxuriousness."[25]

In the essay, *The Conjectural Beginnings of Human History*,[26] Kant remarks that the writers of the ancient scriptures were correct in suggesting that communities immersed in the luxuriousness of the cities, where life is the mere pursuit of pleasure, deserve no better fate than to be wiped from the earth by a universal flood. This sentiment reappears in numerous passages in Kant's work.

In the *Groundwork*, even, Kant remarks that

> if we attend to our experience of the way men act, we meet frequent and, as we ourselves confess, justified complaints that we cannot cite a single sure example of the disposition to act from pure duty.[27]

Thus, an empiricist outlook seems to confirm the fact that men are mere egoists. Because of that fact, Kant says, philosophers have tended to deny the reality of the moral disposition altogether as a sort of pipe-dream. Some have claimed that even though it is "noble enough to take as its precept an idea so worthy of respect," it is certain that none is able to practice it since, "human beings are too frail, corrupt, and weak to follow it."[28] As he laments the sorry state in which men can actually be found, Kant notes that one need not be opposed to moral ideals in order to see the worst in men:

> One need not be an enemy of virtue, but only a cool observer who does not confuse even the liveliest aspiration for the good with its reality, to be doubtful sometimes whether true virtue can really be found anywhere in the world. This is especially true as one's years increase and one's power of judgment is made wiser by experience and more acute in observation.[29]

---

[25]*Beginnings*, 4:339; Beck, p. 65. Kant's biblical references on this page are to Genesis 5:2 and 5:17. Beck has indicated 6:2 and 6:17 in his translation.

[26]Ibid.

[27]*Grundlegung*, 4:263; Beck, p. 22.

[28]Ibid.

[29]*Grundlegung*, 4:264; Beck, p. 24.

From this it is easy to conclude that taking a dim view of things is the result of the relaxation of moral ways of seeing, or the result of the inability to maintain them.

Looked at in a light other than the light of reason, from the point of view of an empirically generated skepticism, human beings appear to be engaged in meaningless activities the ends of which are universal stagnation and folly. The problem, again, is that of how our ordinary perspectives can be revolutionized. What exactly is this revolution and how can it be accomplished? What then does it do for us?

There are two experiences described in detail in Kant's third *Critique* which furnish the material needed to begin a reflection on the problem of how attitudes are revolutionized. These two experiences are of the beautiful and the sublime. The beautiful, according to Kant, is a symbol of the good, the sublime the symbol of "that in contrast with which all else is small."[30] The former is an image of harmony and rest, the latter an image of unimaginable immenseness requiring of its purveyor a struggle to realize the harmony dimly promised by it. The image of the beautiful represents a harmony that awaits the perfection of our moral striving. The image of the sublime represents the incentives driving us to that perfection. They are images of rest and motion.[31]

In moral terms beauty, though representative of the good, induces the pleasure of finality, pleasures which are really self-created. Sublimity, though, offers no grounds for self-satisfied contemplation. In contrast with the sublime, we are small and humbled by its enormity. It seems that there are but two responses called for by the sublime: (a) fascination, and (b) dread. We are alternately spellbound and repelled by it.[32]

What is interesting in Kant's third *Critique* account of the sublime

---

[30]*K3*, 5:321; Meredith, p. 97.

[31]*K3*, 5:329; Meredith, p. 107: "The mind feels itself *set in motion* in the representation of the sublime in nature; whereas in the aesthetic judgment upon what is beautiful therein it is in *restful* contemplation."

[32]Ibid.: "This movement, especially in its inception, may be compared with a vibration, i.e. with a rapidly alternating repulsion and attraction produced by one and the same object."

is that it is said to be a projection of our personalities upon the marvelous things in nature. Kant calls this projection "subreption."[33] What is really sublime is personality, not the immensity of galaxies or the thunderings of volcanoes. Such natural wonders have a peculiar effect upon our consciousnesses. They remind us of the callings of conscience, a power even more immense than anything in nature. Personality is immense simply because it is free from nature, according to Kant. When we catch sight of our power over nature we can then turn our attention away from nature and her powers to direct it upon our own personalities and their vocations.[34]

Sublimity and the Revolution of Perspectives. What we are looking for are some clues to the origin of the revolution in thought required by Kant's moral theory. To be moral and not just to conduct oneself in conformity to the law requires, as we have seen, not the piecemeal refinement of crude attitudes or the gradual elimination of one vice and then another. A Copernican revolution in thought is required, a revolution which fundamentally shifts the orientation of a person from a preoccupation with the inclinations to an attentiveness to the moral law.

Given that the inclinations are naturally attractive as well as powerful, it is clear that something more powerful and attractive will have to be found to produce a turning away from those inclinations. The source of the revolution must be, then, both rational and efficacious. Such a power is described and shown to be essentially related to moral practice in Kant's "Critique of Aesthetic Judgment." This power Kant calls the "sublime."[35]

Kant offers several definitions of the sublime, each of which is, in order, a subtle qualification of the previous one. The most direct

---

[33]Ibid.: "Therefore the feeling of the sublime in nature is respect for our own vocation, which we attribute to an object of nature by a certain subreption (substitution of a respect for the object in place of one for the idea of humanity in our own self—the subject)."

[34]At the end of the second *Critique*, (*KPR*, 5:174; Beck, p. 167), Kant writes: "Two things fill the mind with ever new and increasing admiration and awe the oftener and more steadily we reflect on them: the starry heavens above me and the moral law within me."

[35]*K3*, 5, paragraphs 23-29.

definition of sublimity is "that in contrast with which all else is small."[36] By definition, therefore, there can be nothing greater than the "object" of the sublime. And if something "absolutely great," as Kant calls it, is needed to produce the revolution in a way of thinking, nothing could be found to be more appropriate than the sublime. But what is sublimity and how does Kant show it to be related to his moral philosophy?

The object of the sublime produces in us, Kant says, the feeling of the sublime. This feeling is described primarily as a "cast of mind" produced by the violence done to the subject by his inability to imagine sublime objects.[37] The feeling of the sublime, Kant says, is "the incapacity of the imagination to attain to the idea of the absolutely great," proving that "the imagination is unequal to reason's ideas."[38] This feeling is produced, according to Kant, by the "conflict between the imagination and reason."[39] Thus it differs essentially from the feeling of the beautiful which is produced by the recognition of the harmony between our cognitive faculty (understanding) and the imagination.

The inability of the imagination to attain to an idea of reason is, therefore, the impossibility of representing (imaging) the ideas of reason as *finalities*, or to use Kant's more technical term, *formal finalities*.[40] The sublime is *contra-final*, Kant says.[41] The object of the sublime cannot be represented as beautiful because it cannot be intellectually comprehended as a whole all at once. An object is beautiful if, after some difficulties, one is able to represent it to oneself as a finished product, that is, as one whose image (representation in the imagination) harmonizes with the concepts of the understanding, which means that one is able to intuit all of it at once.

Given that the object of the feeling of the sublime is "that in

---

[36] *K3*, 5:321; Meredith, p. 97.

[37] *K3*, 5:327; Meredith, p. 104.

[38] *K3*, 5:328; Meredith, p. 106.

[39] *K3*, 5:329; Meredith, p. 107.

[40] *K3*, 5:296ff.; Meredith, pp. 69ff.

[41] *K3*, 5:330; Meredith, p. 108.

contrast with which all else is small," it follows that it is infinitely large and that it cannot be represented in an image all at once or, for that matter, at all. Our failed efforts to represent the sublime produce in us, Kant says, a humbling effect. We seem small to ourselves in contrast with it. We recognize in the magnitude of the sublime a power we can never master. Initially, according to Kant, this humbling produces in us fear or terror alternating with fascination. We are drawn toward and then repelled away from the same object.[42]

If our attitudes toward the sublime remain unmediated by *something we can do*, we consequently remain in the state of "vibration" caused by the alternations between dread and fascination.[43] We are freed from this oscillation, according to Kant, "by having a disposition which is upright."[44] This is the connection for which we have been looking. Being morally upright is all we can do to transform the fear of the sublime into respect for it. That this feeling is identified with "moral feeling" is quite clear.[45]

The sublime catches our attention—draws it away from the allurement of the senses—we are fascinated and repelled by a power absolutely great. The oscillations dampen when we begin to act from the incentives generated by the recognition of the sublime object. This happens, according to Kant, only when we give up the effort to represent to ourselves the image of the sublime object. Giving up the attempt to "understand" the object of the sublime, frees us to do that which it commands.[46] Doing that which it commands transforms what had earlier been fear/fascination into an attitude which has been discussed in chapter one: respect. The infinite commands infinitely— we "respect" it as our own rational capacity—and this motivates us to obey it.[47]

---

[42] *K3*, 5:329; Meredith, p. 107.

[43] *K3*, 5:335-36; Meredith, pp. 113-14.

[44] Ibid.

[45] *K3*, 5, paragraph 28, passim.

[46] Ibid.

[47] Ibid.

"Respect," therefore, is the name Kant gives to the post-revolution cast of mind produced by the recognition of the sublime. No longer terrified by sublimity, the moral person "sets manfully to work with full deliberation."[48] He now has a renewed confidence in his ability to free himself from the chains of nature's habits. He is now able to "estimate might without fear and of regarding his estate as exalted above" that of nature's.[49]

It is clear then that Kant's doctrine of the sublime contains a developed notion of the revolution in a man's way of thinking. What is yet to be clarified is the particular nature of the sublime object. The sublime object, as Kant makes clear, is not a natural one. Volcanoes, hurricanes, earthquakes, and so forth invoke the feeling of the sublime by reminding us of the power of *personality* to defy nature:

> the feeling of the sublime in nature is respect for our own vocation, which we attribute to an Object of nature by a certain subreption (substitution of a respect for the Object in place of one for the idea of humanity in our own self—the Subject).[50]

The object of the sublime is, then, personality in ourselves and in the humanity of others. Personality is sublime because (a) it is the source of freedom from nature's laws, and (b) it is the habitat of the moral law.

What produces the revolution in our own ways of thinking is, therefore, our own personalities and the personalities of others—the aspect of the self which gives laws and which dictates what ought to be. It is, of course, just another of Kant's expressions for one and the same power—conscience. The revolution in our way of thinking is produced by the recognition of that in our own selves and the persons of others of that which is worthy of respect—the humanity in each of us. Personality or humanity is itself sublime, according to Kant, because it is

> nothing but the freedom of a rational being under moral laws. . . . Hence it follows that a person is subject to no laws

---

[48] *K3*, 5:334; Meredith, p. 112.

[49] *K3*, 5:336; Meredith, p. 114.

[50] *K3*, 5:329; Meredith, p. 106.

other than those he (either alone or at least jointly with others) gives to himself.[51]

Personality represents man's freedom from the laws of nature, and thus the freedom to obey moral laws. It is the painful recognition of this freedom which produces the revolution in perspectives needed for moral living.

Naiveté, Sublimity, and Morality. The recognition of the sublimity of our own personalities—the freedom from the might of nature—represents the revolution about which much is made in Kant's moral works. The peculiar temper of the resulting cast of mind needs, however, to be given an appropriate description before the relationship between the subjective aspects of Kant's moral theory and the practice of it can be fully clarified. What must be explored are the rather complex descriptions Kant gives of the moral disposition, and the even more puzzling explanations of how this disposition can survive the assaults of the kind of self-consciousness Kant believes is necessary for its maintenance.

It is clear that the proper recognition of the authority of the moral law requires and produces in the subject what Kant calls "humility." Humility is the result of having our "self-love" stricken down by the powerful incentives generated in the recognition of the moral law. This Kant has dwelt upon especially in the second *Critique* in a section entitled, "The Incentives of Pure Practical Reason."[52] In the third *Critique*, however, Kant introduces the notion of "simplicity" to characterize further the "style adopted" by morality. I have mentioned this briefly in chapter one of this essay in connection with the "purification of the moral law." But there is still left the question of what this means exactly.

It will be recalled from chapter one that the passage from the *Groundwork* was mentioned in which Kant noted that "ordinary reason in its practical concern . . . may have as much hope as any philosopher of hitting the mark."[53] The mark Kant is talking about is

---

[51]Ibid.

[52]*KPR*, 5:79ff.; Beck, pp. 74ff.

[53]*Grundlegung*, 4:261; Beck, p. 21. For a discussion of the "style adopted" by morality, cf. *K3*, 5:348; Meredith, p. 128.

the determination of the moral worth of certain actions. Philosophers, in this particular passage, are those whose "judgment is easily confused by a mass of irrelevant considerations."[54] There Kant is expressing his concern that the more subtle a thinker becomes the easier it is for him to quibble with his own conscience. The refined thinker with his educated powers of reflection is clearly presented as one who is likely to over-complicate moral issues by presenting to himself an array of arguments based upon his own selfish interests in favor of courses of action favoring those interests. He will, unlike his "natural" counterpart, have at his disposal an intellectual connoisseurship capable of multiplying his desires, that is, presenting them in the garbs of a pseudo-morality.

The problem with this should now be evident: Kantian morality seems to require for its successful practice an intellectual probity absent from the untutored, but which nevertheless is likely to undermine that which it is supposed to maintain. Intellectual probity is presupposed by the necessity of clarifying the grounds of morality. Without a certain ability to separate the rational from the non-rational sources of motivation, and the intellectual skills to keep them separate (at least in thought), a person is unable to resist some of the more subtle incentives to transgress his duties. Yet the acquisition of those skills brings with it the tendency to create even more subtle "temptations." The question then becomes: how is it possible for a person to be both sophisticated and simple? Or, to put the problem in an even clearer way, how is it possible for a person to be both sophisticated and naive? It seems that a person would have to be both to satisfy fully the demands of Kantian morality, yet it is also clear that these two "styles" are contradictory.[55]

To solve the problem, Kant introduces the notion of a "studied" but not "artificial" naiveté.[56] The successful practice of morality

---

[54]*Grundlegung*, 4:261; Beck, p. 21.

[55]Simplicity Kant defines as "artless finality" in *K3*, 5:348; Meredith, p. 128. This he says is the style of morality. This contradicts the notion of the philosopher in *Grundlegung,* 4:261; Beck, p. 21, who quibbles with his conscience, overcomplicating moral matters.

[56]In *K3*, 5:412; Meredith, p. 203, Kant writes: "for that reason the art of being *naif* is a contradiction. But it is quite possible to give a representation of

requires a curious kind of naïveté, possible only for one who has exercised his intelligence in a special way—a way which must be called a "moral way." But before this is described it must be separated from the "whiz kid" stereotype of the use of intelligence.

The special moral use of intelligence, a use which Kant certainly believes to be the most important use of intelligence, is *not* what might be called the "problem-solving use of intelligence." It is necessary to insist that morality in the practical sense does not require of its practitioners that they be "brains" or "geniuses." Since everyone is obligated to be moral, and since it is clear that not everyone is a genius or a brain, it follows that morality cannot require of its practitioners intellectual brilliance. Nor does it seem to require any particular skill in making subtle logical deductions from principles. Kant insists repeatedly that morality is possible for all. In this Kant seems to differ from Plato.

Clarity of moral vision is not the product of subtle intellectual ratiocination.[57] It is, instead, the product of the purity of intentions, or as Kant puts it in the *Groundwork*, a good will. What this seems to mean is that what we in our age have come to term intelligence—the ability to solve difficult problems quickly; to memorize complicated formulae and information; to be quick-witted; to be clever; and to be able to carry on a subtle train of thought—is not what Kant has in mind when he is speaking of moral intelligence. So, what then is it?

Moral intelligence, for Kant, it may be argued, is primarily the ability to free oneself from duplicity in one's way of thinking. It is nothing but "truthfulness and straightforwardness in one's way of thinking." Kant calls this "sincerity."[58] Now what is curious is that people who are sincere in Kant's sense of that term are people who are usually accused of "not being wise after the manner of men."[59] They appear to be unwise because they appear to be "simpletons," and

---

naïveté in a fictitious personage, and, rare as the art is, it is a fine art." Kant evidently believes the moral *posture* to be similar—it is *studied naïveté*.

[57] Cf. *K3*, 5, paragraph 49, and *KPR*, 5, p. 176; Beck, p. 167.

[58] *Theodicee*, 6:130; Despland, p. 290.

[59] *K3*, 5:412; Meredith, p. 203.

"naifs".[60] They have a certain otherworldly appearance in that they seem to be uninterested in the preoccupations of sophisticates. They seem also to be unfashionable characters whose lives are "artless."[61] In the presence of such "naifs" our own postures are revealed to be corrupt.

> Outward appearance, fair but false, that usually assumes such importance in our judgment, is here, at a stroke, turned to a nullity—the rogue in us is nakedly exposed, calls forth a movement of the mind in two successive and opposite directions, agitating the body at the same time with wholesome motion.[62]

We realize in the presence of moral purity that our own lives and attitudes, especially the sophisticated ones, are pretentious and shallow.

> But that something infinitely better than any accepted code of manners, namely purity of mind (or at least a vestige of such purity), has not become wholly extinct in human nature infuses seriousness and reverence into this play of judgment. . . . When it becomes covered over again there enters into the above feeling a touch of pity.[63]

The connection between moral purity and naiveté is made clearer yet in an earlier passage from the same section of the third *Critique*.

> Naiveté is the breaking forth of the ingenuousness originally natural to humanity, in opposition to the art of disguising oneself that has become a second nature. We laugh at the simplicity that is as yet a stranger to dissimulation, but we rejoice the while over the simplicity of nature that thwarts that art. We await the commonplace manner of artificial utterance, thoughtfully addressed to a fair show, and lo! nature stands before us in unsullied innocence—nature that

---

[60]Ibid.

[61]*K3*, 5:348; Meredith, p. 128.

[62]*K3*, 5:411-12; Meredith, p. 202.

[63]Ibid.

we were quite unprepared to meet, and that he who laid it bare had also no intention of revealing.[64]

Naiveté, since it thwarts the art of disguising oneself—an art which Kant here calls a "second nature"—is here quite similar to a moral purity which prevents one from lying to oneself.[65] Moral purity is willing one thing, the good. The good will is simple just to the extent that it wills one thing and not many. The necessity of producing that simplicity in our own ways of thinking is emphasized by Kant in many different places in his work, though nowhere quite so clearly as in the first section of the *Groundwork*.[66]

Morality, for Kant, is really a self-induced straightforwardness of mind which defeats our inclination to overcomplicate the directness of the demands of the moral law. This is why one wants to call it a strange mixture of sophistication and naiveté. Here again Kant is walking a fine line between extremes. He is all too suspicious of what he calls the "extravagancies of genius,"[67] wants to insist that genius is not required for moral living, yet is also certain that special efforts are required for such a life, efforts which appear to be absent from the lives of the "naturally good." The two extreme figures would be then the genius and the saint. The one is too sophisticated, the other is too simple, though both are admirable in their own special ways. The problem with both figures is that they owe their facilities to nature and not to effort. One must, it seems, be born to either genius or sainthood. Neither has genuinely made himself into what he is, and consequently his "talents" cannot be requirements for moral living. The moral posture is a posture which is peculiarly self-made and can therefore be considered to have moral worth.

Morality, we might say, is a self-constructed attitude wrought from elements common to both genius and saintliness. The moral man must self-consciously "invent" his life just as the genius freely originates his works of art. Yet he must also self-consciously create in

---

[64]Ibid.

[65]Ibid.

[66]*Grundlegung*, 4:261; Beck, p. 21.

[67]*KPR*, 5:176; Beck, p. 167.

himself a will which is good, a will which the saint seems to have naturally. The moral man self-consciously pursues moral goals with the originality of genius and the singlemindedness of the saint. This is the texture of Kantian moral living. This is just another example of what I had been pointing out in the section on the wire-walker. The moral man Kant pictures lives his life out of attitudes which are self-induced and must be constantly maintained. Since he is neither a genius nor a saint, he stays on the wire by virtue of an effort of will. The act of will here is not, to use Iris Murdoch's phrase, a "flash of the will."[68] It appears in the life of the moral person as an attitude enduring even between ethical crises, which gives a "mood" to his whole life.

---

[68] Murdoch, *The Sovereignty of Good,* p. 53: "The agent, thin as a needle, appears in the quick flash of the choosing will." Murdoch criticizes this characterization of moral activity.

Chapter Five

A Kantian
Moral Biography

In this chapter the focus will be changed. The purpose here is to move from the earlier discussions of moral attitudes, dispositions, and perspectives toward an understanding of the kind of life, and not just the kinds of actions, that could be expected of someone who is moral in Kant's sense of that term. There are problems with the interpretation of Kant's moral philosophy that can only be resolved by addressing two aspects of what might be called the standard interpretation of Kantian morality. Once these peculiarities of the standard view of Kant's philosophy are identified and presented in a sort of bold relief, the significance of the reinterpretation can be clearly seen.

In the history of philosophy there is a marked tendency for thinkers to suppose that human action is meaningless unless it moves towards already clarified goals. Indeed, the distinction between action and behavior is often made by saying that actions are purposive (goal-oriented), while behaviors are not. Behaviors are movements, either bodily or mental, that are caused by something other than an agent's own conscious intentions. Thus the behavior of snoring, for example, is not intended by the agent. It is simply the consequence of certain physiological factors over which the agent has no direct control. It is true that people are often blamed for snoring by those who are subjected to the nuisance. Blaming such behavior does not, unfortunately, extinguish it, since the snorer, though he may genuinely regret his behavior, can do nothing about it at the time it occurs. This is not to say that snoring cannot be stopped. There are programs of conditioning to which the sleeper may be subjected: programs designed to alter the behavior either mechanically or organically. It must be controlled, therefore, by something other than the agent's own conscious efforts. The point here is that behaviors, like snoring, are non-purposive. They do not move toward consciously held objectives. Actions do, or at least they are thought to, move toward consciously held objectives. This is often thought to be the case with a whole life as well. Lives, we suppose, can be managed in much the same way that actions are.

One can decide what one wants to do with one's own life. One can make plans to be an aeronautical engineer, a physicist, a teacher, or a city planner. One can then take steps to realize those plans. One can, that is, attempt to organize one's life toward certain long-term ends. Once one has committed oneself to such a plan, or to such long-term ends, one is then committed, as well, to the means to the realizations of them. And it is often the case that as the agent moves toward his long-term goal, the goal itself is transformed. When we decide to pursue some particular course of life, that course begins to appear to have changed as we move through it toward its ultimate intention. This can be explained by saying that the particular activities that must fill that life with content also produce, upon reflection, different evaluations of the significance of that life. We can say, as well, that the significance of particular actions is colored by the overall conception of a course of life.

There is a peculiar kind of reciprocity between the actions in a life and the conception of what that whole life is about. Actions transform the conception of the goals of a whole life, and the goals of a whole life charge particular actions with a significance they would not otherwise have. This reciprocity is one of the conditions of life which is not fully appreciated by moralists who suppose that lives consist fully of a sequence of separately good actions. The end of life, according to this abstract account of it, is some kind of good conduct. A life is good just to the extent that its separate episodes are good. Efforts are therefore made to ascertain just which actions are good and which are bad so that the good may be done and the bad avoided. But what I would argue is that a life lived in this way is not a life at all, but a sequence of routines. A moral philosophy which neglects the reflective dimensions of human life does not deserve to be called a moral philosophy at all.

The significance of Kant's moral philosophy is usually ignored by students of philosophy. What is remarkable about Kant's moral philosophy is that it presents its readers with what in his day was a new and more comprehensive picture of moral living, a picture of a course of life open to rational agents which is neither purposeless, nor determined in all of its facets by objective insights. The center of the Kantian notion of moral life is not, therefore, a goal which is objectively determinable by the apprehension of eternal verities, but, instead, a coherent set of guiding principles—principles to which rational agents may look for guidance. And most importantly, Kant's conception of moral life is not wedded to either rationalistic or empirical conceptions of natural ends.

Kant's conception of moral life is a conception that is animated by a revolutionary notion of teleology. Prior to Kant's work, philosophers and lay people alike supposed that either one must organize one's life in accordance with churchly conceptions of it, or one must organize one's life in accordance with various interpretations of the workings of nature. The alternatives were life in accordance with supernatural ends, or life in accordance with natural ends. The Kantian teleology prescribes a life in accordance with freedom. But what does that mean? Can there be such a thing as a "free teleology"? And if so, what is it?

A "free teleology" would be a teleology animated by what Kant calls "the laws of freedom." The laws of freedom are defined by Kant as "moral laws." Moral laws are laws in accordance with which things ought to happen, allowing for conditions under which what ought to happen often does not. What this means is that a teleology of freedom would be a teleology which specifies *how* self-chosen goals are to be pursued, but does not specify *which* goals should be pursued. A free agent, in Kant's sense, is an agent who freely chooses his own goals, but who is limited in the pursuit of those goals by the moral laws and by the conditions under which what ought to happen often does not. The limitations on rational endeavor are, therefore, moral constraints which are adopted freely, and natural constraints over which the agent has no control.

X may not murder Y, not because his community or his society makes murder illegal or says that it is immoral, but because the murder of Y destroys Y's prerogatives entirely—it negates that which X values both in himself and in others. Murder is wrong because it destroys freedom, and since it destroys freedom it destroys the supremacy of the moral laws themselves. Y may not jump to the moon, not because there are moral limitations on his endeavor, but because there are natural limitations over which Y has no control. Moral agents must be aware of both moral and natural limitations on rational endeavor. The awareness of these limitations is what has been described throughout the first four chapters above. The consciousness of both the moral and the natural limitations on rational endeavor just *is* morality, for Kant. And a picture of the efficacy of this consciousness on the life of a person would show what shape a moral life would have. It would provide, as well, an illustration of an agent's gradual realization that his own life both can and should be self-managed. It would show just the extent to which natural (biological) teleologies in fact operate in the course of life, and it would show what sort of responses to their effects would be possible for rational agents.

To present a moral biography, we may make use of four of Kant's later essays. We shall provide an imaginative interpretation of each to represent the most important aspects of the total course of human life. It is not the intention here to suggest that the sketches are accurate expositions of the complex themes presented in Kant's later essays. The intention, instead, is to use materials from Kant's works to show that he was fully aware of the reflective dimensions of the totality of human life. After these sketches, a short summary is offered in which the significance of the enterprise will be made clear.[1]

---

[1]The "growth" industries seem to rest upon the assumption that consciousness grows and develops similarily to the human body. Thus, the stages in mental development are said to parallel the stages in physical development. Even if this is an accurate account of human life it does not

The Beginnings of Human History and Biography

Conjectural Beginnings of Human History,[2] in the English translation, is but sixteen pages in length. In this document the thesis is double-edged: first, that the blame for the many moral evils men suffer in their lives can be laid at their own doorsteps, and secondly, that the ancient part of history teaches that man should be content with Providence—that is, with the course of human history *taken as a whole*. The support Kant gives these claims takes the form of a narrative based upon a rational reinterpretation of chapters two to six of *Genesis*.[3]

In this sacred work Kant finds materials for what he calls a "pleasure trip" through the earliest stages of human history, stages the knowledge of which is absent, but about which some clues are available since they can be "rationally derived from experience." What Kant achieves here "undertaken on the wings of the imagination," is the *temporalization of the major tenets of his moral theory*.[4] His readers are given, in effect, the *conjectured biographies* of the first human beings—Adam and Eve.

Kant's use of the term "conjectured" is surely an irony of no small proportions. *Genesis*, chapters 2-6, though often interpreted by naive

---

follow that rational beings become more and more obligated to obey the moral law, or that at certain early stages of development they are not bound by its dictates. If the various psychologistic accounts of mental development are accurate they could amount to no more than plots of human frailty, at least from the moral point of view. Though a person may claim either retardation or advancement from the normal developmental schedules and thus claim such as an *excuse* for moral failure, he cannot claim an *exemption*.

Kant's own account of moral growth, its various stages, is a record of the appearance of reason in life and the responses of the subject to these appearances.

[2] *Beginnings.*

[3] Even by today's standards of biblical scholarship Kant's interpretation of *Genesis* would have to be considered revisionary. He does not, for example, suppose that *Genesis* is an actual account of the beginning of the universe, nor does he even offer literal interpretation of its various episodes.

[4] Kant discusses the gradual appearance of reason in human life, its different effects on rational beings at different stages of moral development.

readers as an actual account of the first human couple, is for Kant the narrative reconstruction, or perhaps better still, the retrogressive projection of the necessary stages of the moral development of every rational being. The *Genesis* story embodies, for Kant, an archetypical pattern of the gradual emergence of reason as a power that gives man freedom from the natural inclinations.[5] It is therefore the *mythos* giving a temporal shape to the presuppositions of morality.

The irony, to be sure, is that only the concrete personalities of Adam and Eve, the vivid descriptions of the garden of Eden, and the seductive advances of the snake are *conjectured*. All the rest, the rational patterns embodied in these vivid images, can be found in the earliest stages of the lives of each and every human being. As such, Kant's account of *Genesis*, chapters 2-6, is not an account of the beginnings of human history, but instead the beginnings of every single human story. It is less significant, then, as a story of human history than as the beginning of a moral biography. I shall therefore present the skeletal version of Kant's account of moral progress so that the reader will be able to appreciate the intimate connections between Kant's "conjectures" and his earlier critical doctrines.

Kant says that his "sole purpose is to consider the development of manners and morals in Man's way of life,"[6] and to that end he supposes man to have already certain skills, for example, the abilities to stand, walk, speak, discourse, and to think in coherent concepts. Yet in the beginning the moral novice is guided by instinct alone, an instinct which, Kant asserts, is a "voice of God which is obeyed by all animals."[7] The voice of instinct is said to have provided man with all of his natural needs. He could, with its help, distinguish between those things which are helpful and harmful to his physical well-being. The animal, according to Kant, consumes only that which is necessary for its health and instinctively rejects food which might prove harmful.

As long as man "obeyed the call of nature all was well with him."[8]

---

[5] The gradual appearance of reason parallels, not biological developments, but the gradual awaking of freedom in human life.

[6] *Beginnings*, 4:329; Beck, p. 55.

[7] Ibid.

[8] Ibid.

Kant is here referring to the state of the first couple in the garden prior to the fall. "But soon reason began to stir."[9] Reason is presented in this account as a power gradually *insinuating itself* into the activities of men; first, Kant suggests, into "a sense different from that to which instinct was tied."[10] The sense of sight, Kant suggests, notices foodstuffs not ordinarily consumed, and reason, "instituting a comparison, sought to enlarge its knowledge"[11] beyond the bounds of instinct. Reason thus appears first as a power that "with the aid of the imagination" can create artificial desires which are not only unsupported by natural instinct but actually contrary to it."[12]

Desires multiplied endlessly by the imagination then, according to Kant, "generate a whole host of unnecessary and indeed unnatural inclinations called luxuriousness."[13] Once, under the guidance of instinct alone, man did not need to choose between natural goods and those created by his imagination. Now with the arrival of the power to create a supermarket of artificial foods, man is in the awkward position of having to choose between them. He may either follow his instinct or choose not to.

Given the first opportunity to choose, an opportunity represented by Eve's temptation to choose "a fruit which tempted because of its similarity to tasty fruits of which man had already partaken,"[14] an understandable mistake was made. But this mistake, which, since men were not practiced in choosing, could not have been avoided, was "a sufficient occasion for reason to do violence to the voice of nature and, its protest notwithstanding, to make the first attempt at free choice."[15] This first free choice, according to Kant, demonstrated to man that he had the power to choose against his natural instinct, and was therefore

---

[9]Ibid.

[10]Ibid.

[11]Ibid.

[12]Ibid., 4:330; Beck, p. 56.

[13]Ibid.

[14]Ibid.

[15]Ibid.

of monumental significance for later moral development. For without that freedom to choose against instinct man could never choose for himself a way of life different from that to which his nature has previously bound him.

> But however insignificant the damage done, it sufficed to open man's eyes (3:7). He discovered in himself a power of choosing for himself a way of life, of not being bound without alternative to a single way, like the animals. Perhaps the discovery of this advantage created a moment of delight. But of necessity, anxiety and alarm as to how he was to deal with this newly discovered power quickly followed; for man was a being who did not yet know either the secret properties or the remote effects of anything. He stood, as it were, at the brink of an abyss.[16]

This first choice is, according to Kant, a turning point in the life of man. When once it is reached it commits him necessarily to his new state, a state from which he cannot return to his former life of instinct.

The next few stages in man's moral development consist largely of new manifestations of the power of reason over instinct. The fig leaf, for example, is, according to Kant, "a greater manifestation of reason than that shown in the earlier stages of development."[17] It represents the mastery man has over the sexual instinct, an instinct which is greatly magnified by the imagination. The mastery of this instinct makes possible the step from "merely sensual to spiritual attraction, from mere animal desire gradually to love."[18] The power manifested by the fig leaf, then, is, according to Kant, the power of *refusal*. In this power there is to be found "a first hint at the development of man as a moral creature."[19]

This first hint of morality Kant calls "a sense of decency."[20] It is defined as an "inclination to inspire others to respect by proper

---

[16]Ibid.

[17]Ibid., 4:331; Beck, p. 57.

[18]Ibid.

[19]Ibid.

[20]Ibid.

manners, i.e., by concealing all that which might arouse low esteem."[21] The sense of decency contains, Kant says, "the real basis of all true sociability."[22] It is clear, though, that manners alone are not genuine morality, and the powers to refuse or to conceal need still be developed through some other stages before they can be shown to precede genuine morality.

So far there have been two stages of development. The first was the subjection to instinct, the second a discovery of the mastery one has over one's instincts. The third, however, gives a sense of wholeness to man's life. It is, as Kant puts it, "the conscious expectation of the future."[23] At the same time, one is given the ability to plan for the future, to make distant goals a present preoccupation, and to fear death. Though men look forward to their projects with a sense of hope, they begin to wonder whether this advantage is a blessing when they realize that their plans must sometime come to a speedy end in death. Men begin, therefore, Kant says, to decry "as a crime the use of reason, which had been the cause of all these ills."[24] But they are consoled partially by the "prospect of living through their children who might enjoy a better future, or else hope that these latter members of their family might alleviate their burden."[25]

The last step which reason took was to give man the understanding that he alone was the true end of nature, that he is raised infinitely above the sheep and the goats, and more importantly, that *all men are his equal in this*. The last step is, therefore, the step which assures man that his rational neighbors are his equals. It prepares him to construct a system of restraints binding on himself and to regulate his relationships with others. Kant refers, paternally, one supposes, to this as man's "release from the womb of nature."[26] Man was driven, finally, from his comfortable childhood in the garden "into the wide world,

---

[21] Ibid.

[22] Ibid.

[23] Ibid.

[24] Ibid., 4:332; Beck, p. 58.

[25] Ibid.

[26] Ibid., 4:333; Beck, p. 59.

where so many cares, troubles, and unforeseen ills awaited him."[27]
This represents, of course, the rite of initiation to adulthood where
man must

> take up patiently the toil which he yet hates, and pursue the
> frippery which he despises. It would make him forget even
> death itself which he dreads, because of all those trifles
> which he is even more afraid to lose.[28]

Kant's conjectures about the beginnings of human history contain,
therefore, an account of the earliest stages of moral development
represented in the following sequence: (1) The initial appearance of
man in the garden—the womb of nature—where all of his needs are
taken care of by a benevolent (one might even say an *amniotic*) nature.
(2) The beginning of man's naive use of his capacity to choose against
his nature—a use which brings with it the freedom to make mistakes
which, though inconsequential in the beginning, contains the seeds of
what later will become the ground of his own character. Kant defines
character as that which man makes of himself, in contrast to that
which nature makes of man. This stage represents also the first
awakening of man's imagination, foreshadowing his eventual capacity
to live toward goals that he creates for himself. *Refusal*, Kant says, is
man's power to act contrary to his nature.

In man's refusal there is born a nascent reflectivity, making it
possible for man to *hide* himself from others. This ability, called a
"sense of decency," is the ground for what Kant calls "sociability."[29] It
must be noted that the "sense of decency" is closely related to man's
ability also to hide from himself. Paradoxically, the concealment that
makes good-mannered social life a possibility is also the same thing
which generates most of the personal and social ills.[30] Self-
concealment is a self-conceit against which the genuinely moral man
spends most of his efforts in attempts at self-revelation. Self-

---

[27]Ibid.

[28]Ibid.

[29]Ibid., 4:331; Beck, p. 57.

[30]Cf. Emil Fackenheim, "Kant and Radical Evil," *University of Toronto Quarterly* 23 (1953-54).

revelation, when successful, is what Kant calls, in *Theodicy*, "sincerity."[31] Sincerity is there said to be the ground of all of the other virtues. Its opposite, worthlessness, destroys morality by undermining its foundations.

(3) The third stage in man's moral development is the awakening of "the conscious expectation of the future." This makes it possible, clearly, for man to plan a way of life as well as to fear the end of his projects in his own death. This stage, as will be argued later, is really significant, because it makes possible the reflective survey of the whole of life.

(4) The fourth and final stage is that in which man becomes aware of his moral worth over against the other animals. In his "release from the womb of nature" he is condemned, we might say, to regulate his conduct with his fellows who are his own moral equals. It is here that he finally realizes that he must labor toward goals legislated for him by his own reason in a social setting where others similarly labor toward goals which are often opposed to his. He learns to tolerate others, to respect their endeavors, and to communicate his own projects candidly to those who will probably oppose him.[32]

This last stage, since it is so clearly representative of one's passage into adulthood, a stage in which one spends most of one's life, needs special attention at this point. Kant's treatment of this theme, since it is a central preoccupation of many of the moral writings, and since it presents special interpretive problems, must be examined carefully. What is especially interesting about Kant's analysis of the passage into adulthood is that the passage is not presented as irreversible.[33] One may, it appears, enter adulthood and then for various reasons regress to what appear to be earlier stages of moral development. One does not, of course, grow younger as one regresses. But what is clear is that the moral attitudes one must adopt in adult life are not self-sustaining. Moral attitudes, as presented earlier in this essay, can, if not properly maintained, collapse into others which must be described as

---

[31] *Theodicee*, 6:130; Desplant, p. 290.

[32] *Beginnings,* 4:337-39; Beck, pp. 63-65.

[33] Ibid., 4:333; Beck, p. 59.

pathological regressions.[34] In *Conjectural Beginnings* Kant summarizes the above point in a single passage:

> In the future, the wretchedness of his condition would often arouse in him the wish for a paradise, the creation of his imagination, where he could dream or while away his existence in quiet inactivity and permanent peace.[35]

If we represent adulthood in Kantian terms as toil and frippery[36]— a labor necessary for the development of talents and the development of those social graces needed to live morally with our antagonists—the tendency to recoil from the struggles of adult life will also have to be given a description. Kant presents his readers with at least two different *pathologies of retreat*. The first is mysticism and the second is empiricism.

If we consider mysticism or empiricism from the point of view of their *temporal dimensions*—if one looks at them, that is, in the context of moral development—one is certain to notice that each exhibits an interesting pattern. The mystic and the empiricist, along with all other human beings, had been expelled from the garden of childhood at the time "reason was awakened." However, the mystic and the empiricist each develop different strategies for recapturing what they had lost prior to the "fall." The mystic, pictured by Kant in *The End of All Things*[37] as "the brooding man,"[38] creates an imaginary paradise in which, since there is no change, he may while away his time in the quiet contemplation of eternal verities. His progress is abruptly halted as he reaches for the glittering creations of his own imagination. His life is to be characterized primarily as *suspended out of time*.

---

[34]Pathological in the sense that Kant uses the term: one is *naturally inclined* to wish for a return to an "Arcadian shepherd's life," for example.

[35]*Beginnings*, 4:333; Beck, p. 59.

[36]Ibid.: *"Sie treibt ihn an, die Mühe, die er hasst, dennoch geduldig über sich zu nehmen, dem Flitterwerk, das er verachtet, nachzulaufen, und den Tod selbst, vor dem ihn gravet, über alle jene Kleinigkeiten, deren Verlust er noch mehr scheuet, zu vergessen."*

[37]*Ende.*

[38]*Ende*, 6:420; Beck, p. 79: "nachgrübelnde Mensch in die Mystik."

The empiricist, in order to escape a steady progress, creates for himself a life chiefly characterized by a series of backslidings. Thus in his life there is the repetition of one who is constantly trying and then failing to gratify different desires. Though he is not suspended out of time, he nevertheless makes of his life a *regressive spiral*, each cycle or oscillation of which takes him closer to the currents of nature; a nature in which the incentives of reason are progressively weakened as its own hold grows more powerful.

Samuel Johnson, in his "Vision of Theodore, Hermit of Teneriffe,"[39] creates a nearly perfect picture of the regressive spiral of the empiricist. It is quoted here to consolidate the various descriptions of the empiricist offered elsewhere above.

> There were others . . . who retreated from the heat and tumult of the way, . . . They wandered on from one double of the labyrinth to another with the chains of Habit hanging secretly upon them, till, as they advanced, the flowers grew paler, and the scents fainter; they proceeded in their dreary march without pleasure in their progress, yet without power to return; and had this aggravation above all others, that they were criminal but not delighted. The drunkard for a time laughed over his wine; the ambitious man triumphed in the miscarriage of his rival; but the captives of Indolence had neither superiority nor merriment. Discontent lowered in their looks, and sadness hovered round their shades; yet they arrived at the depth of the recess, varied only with poppies and nightshade, where the dominion of Indolence terminates, and the hopeless wanderer is delivered up to Melancholy; the chains of Habit are rivetted forever; and Melancholy, having tortured her prisoner for a time, consigns him at last to the cruelty of Despair.[40]

In this sketch one is able to see again the same pattern as that which emerged in the picture presented of David Hume in chapter one above.

---

[39]"Visions of Theodore, Hermit of Teneriffe," in *The Works of Samuel Johnson*, A New Edition in Twelve Volumes (London: Luke Hanfard, 1806), 2:454-71.

[40]Ibid., 2:469-70.

What is clear is that the spiral descent is a retreat from "the heat and tumult of the way." "The existence of such yearnings," Kant writes,

> proves that thoughtful persons weary of civilized life, if they seek its value in pleasure alone, and if, reminded by reasons that they might give value to life by actions, fall back on laziness, to counteract this reminder. But this wish for a return to an age of simplicity and innocence is futile. The foregoing presentation of man's original state teaches us that, because he could not be satisfied with it man could not remain in this state, much less be inclined ever to return to it; that therefore he must, after all, ascribe his present troublesome condition to himself and his own choice.[41]

When Kant asserts, as he does in *Conjectural Beginnings*, that man is free, unlike the animals, to choose a way of life, he clearly means that one is free to regress as well as to progress. By surveying one's own life, its future and its past, one recognizes that, though one must naturally grow older and die, one also is able to live that life either toward the future or toward the past. One has, therefore, the freedom either to attempt to recreate the garden in various ways which end in failure, or to labor toward an open and, therefore, either a hopeful or a dreadful future.[42]

The *Idea of a Universal History*

If Kant's *Conjectural Beginnings of Human History* provides readers with a temporal mythos about the gradual emergence of reason in human life, then his *Idea of a Universal History* supplies them with an account of the workings of reason in adult life and a characterization of the interactions between persons in a cosmopolitan setting. Kant here presents his account of adult life in the form of the following nine theses:[43]

---

[41] *Beginnings,* 4:341; Beck, p. 68.

[42] Cf. *Beginnings*, 4:331-32; Beck, pp. 57-58.

[43] *Idea*, 4, (1) p. 152, (2) p. 153, (3) p. 154, (4) p. 155, (5) p. 156, (6) p. 157, (7) p. 158, (8) p. 161, (9) p. 164; Beck, (1) p. 12, (2) p. 13, (3) p. 13, (4) p. 15, (5) p. 16, (6) p. 17, (7) p. 18, (8) p. 21, (9) p. 23.

1. *All natural capacities of a creature are destined to evolve completely to their natural end.*
2. *In man (as the only rational creature on earth) those natural capacities which are directed to the use of his reason are to be fully developed only in the race, not in the individual.*
3. *Nature has willed that man should be himself, produce everything that goes beyond the mechanical ordering of his animal existence, and that he should partake of no other happiness or perfection than that which he himself, independently of instinct, has created by his own reason.*
4. *The means employed by Nature to bring about the development of all the capacities of man is their antagonism in society, so far as this is, in the end, the cause of a lawful order among men.*
5. *The greatest problem for the human race, to the solution of which Nature drives man, is the achievement of a universal civic society which administers law among men.*
6. *This problem is the most difficult and the last to be solved by mankind.*
7. *The problem of establishing a perfect civic constitution is dependent upon the problem of a lawful external relation among states and cannot be solved without a solution of the latter problem.*
8. *The history of mankind can be seen, in the large, as the realization of Nature's secret plan to bring forth a perfectly constituted state as the only condition in which the capacities of mankind can be fully developed, and also bring forth that external relation among states which is perfectly adequate to this end.*
9. *A philosophical attempt to work out a universal history according to a natural plan directed to achieving the civic union of the human race must be regarded as possible and, indeed, as contributing to this end of Nature.*

From these nine theses, many of which have only an indirect bearing on Kant's moral philosophy (they are central to his philosophy of history), it is possible to construct an interesting portrait of adult life, three features of which need to be mentioned. The first is Kant's notion of social antagonism contained in thesis four; the second, the idea that the natural capacities of mankind are developed fully only in the race and not in the individual; and the third, the importance of the ideal of a secret plan of Nature, which, by means of social antagonisms, advances the species toward its natural end, that is, a federation of states under universal laws.

The first needs discussion because of its recognition of the fact that adult life consists not in the harmony of individuals in society, but in the conflict between them. Kant is not, of course, arguing that individuals *ought* to be antagonistic to each other. He is recognizing the fact that they are. Kant calls antagonism "the unsocial sociability of men" (*ungesellige Geselligkeit der Menschen*).[44] For, as he writes,

> man has an inclination to associate with others, because in society he feels himself to be more than man, i.e., as more than the developed form of his natural capacities. But he also has a strong propensity to isolate himself from others, because he finds in himself at the same time the unsocial characteristic of wishing to have everything go according to his own wish. Thus he expects opposition on all sides because, in knowing himself, he knows that he, on his own part, is inclined to oppose others. This opposition it is which awakens all his powers, brings him to conquer his inclination to laziness and, propelled by vainglory, lust for power, and avarice, to achieve a *rank among his fellows whom he cannot tolerate but from whom he cannot withdraw.*[45]

Without such antagonism, according to Kant, man's natural capacities

> would remain hidden, unborn in an Arcadian shepherd's life, with all its concord, contentment, and mutual affection. Men, good-natured as the sheep they herd, would hardly reach a higher worth than their beasts; they would not fill the empty place in creation by achieving their end, which is rational nature.[46]

---

[44]*Idea*, 4:155; Beck, p. 15.

[45]Ibid., emphasis mine.

[46]*Idea*, 4:155-56; Beck, pp. 15-16.

It is only in the childhood of both the species and the individual that there is "concord, contentment, and mutual affection."[47] Adulthood consists of the opposite of this Arcadian existence. Kant pictures adulthood primarily as misery and strife within, and because of, social antagonisms. Morality must be considered, therefore, at least partially, as the disposition first to *tolerate*, and then to *respect* the persons of those with whom one is in continuous conflict. Morality, in adult life, expresses itself in two distinct stages: the first is the practice of good manners; the second, a development of good disposition. Good manners, that is, civility, is the soil—the womb—in which genuine morality develops gradually. Genuine morality—an inner disposition or outlook—consists of the recognition of the differences in the ends people set for themselves, their rights to such ends, and the will to attempt to harmonize their various ends with each other. Good manners is merely the *show* of such recognition, morality is that recognition itself.[48]

The Kingdom of Ends, as pictured in the *Groundwork*, is the ideal of a social world in which apparently contradictory ends are represented as socially compossible.[49] Treating persons as ends-in-themselves consists, therefore, in recognizing precisely in which respects we differ from them, respecting those differences, and working toward their harmonization with good will.

Morality consists, therefore, of a series of imputations. Each person must be considered as a person who, (a) knows what he wants, (b) intends to get it, (c) is willing to discuss with others what he wants and how he intends to get it, and (d) recognizes the limitations imposed on his own endeavors by the social setting, i.e., that his ends must be compossible with the ends of others.[50] They are definitive of the good will in a social setting, and as such, can be considered to be the

---

[47]Ibid.

[48]Cf. *Idea*, 4:161; Beck, p. 21.

[49]Cf. *Grundlegung*, 4:297-99; Beck, pp. 56-58.

[50]See Kant's discussion of the proper use of the cognitive powers in *Anthropologie*, 8:117-18; Gregor, pp. 95-97. Much of what I am arguing here is based upon Kant's "maxims for thinkers."

concretizations of the categorical imperative.[51]

The interesting implication here is that morality is the willingness of a person to communicate his own ends to others and to discuss those ends openly. This all would be impossible without the presupposition of self-knowledge, the imputations of (a) and (b) above. Yet there is here, as elsewhere in Kant, the intimate connection of self-knowledge with knowledge of other.[52]

A person, in adult life, comes to know himself as he discusses his purposes with others. He "constructs" himself in a social setting and his character, therefore, reflects the products and procedures of dialogue. Each person, though he must make himself, must make himself in a social context in accordance with (or rather, for the sake of) universal moral rules binding, by definition, on all. He is free there to construct a "self" that is moral, which means that he is free to construct a "self" for which he is willing to be socially responsible. What he constructs, therefore, will be, or ought to be, a reflection of the rational demands of the larger social setting.

Now this picture of adult life is, I think, quite different from the one imagined so often by some of Kant's critics, especially those who imagine moral life in Kant's sense to be a dreary, even if rational, monotony of doing a series of routine duties.[53] It may well be that if everyone were perfectly rational, that is, if the purposes of each and every person were *in fact* compossible, life would be monotonous just to the extent that there would be nothing to dispute and consequently nothing about which to think or converse. However, such a social

---

[51] *In practice* morality can be considered to be the adoption of respectful attitudes towards others whose wants and purposes run counter to ours. Our moral duties with respect to them change not at all regardless of how antagonistic they may be to our own pursuits.

[52] I am here noting the extent to which self-revelation is a function of dialogue. I do not think that Kant underestimated the importance of it. See his discussion of the importance of communities of belief in *Religion*; his many discussions of social gatherings, discourse and even dining in *Anthropologie*. A thorough treatment of this topic would require a separate study for which there is no room here.

[53] For an example of this sort of misunderstanding of Kant see Iris Murdoch's treatment of Kant in *The Sovereignty of Good*.

world is ruled out *a priori* for rational creatures who are, by definition, finite.[54] That is why Kant insists that talents are to be fully developed not in individuals, but in the race as a whole.

Individuals make singular contributions to the idea of a perfect social unity not by *being* perfect, but by openly sharing their differences with others whose purposes are opposite and contradictory. Most legal and moral principles are limitations on contest.[55] They define quite precisely within which limitations debate must proceed. A person is *civil* if he *observes* these limitations, and *moral* if he *takes* them *to heart*.[56] The moral adult person recognizes (and accepts) the demand that his conduct (the pursuit of his ends) be rationally justifiable—that it be open to discussion.

Kant's picture of adult moral life in *The Idea of a Universal History* is considerably richer in nuances than the *Groundwork* picture. If we are to think of the whole of life as stretching between two childhoods encompassing adolescence, adulthood and old age, then we can think of moral life as proceeding through three distinct stages: demand, alienation and reconciliation.[57] Adulthood, as Kant pictures it in *Idea*, is alienation, that is, antagonism, and the effort to reconcile our purposes with the purposes of others while at the same time obeying and then taking to heart the principles governing contest and argumentation. As Ward puts it:

---

[54] *Idea*, 4:153; Beck, p. 13.

[55] This follows from the fact that agreements cannot easily be reached by opposing parties, and that since opposition is the chief characteristic of adult life, as Kant portrays it, rules for how to treat adversaries (indeed, how to think of them) are required. These rules are moral laws, not just good manners.

[56] Kant believed that after a lengthy period of education the rational person adopts as his own the spirit of the laws with which he had been merely oppressed before he came to understand them. Kant's *Lectures on Pedagogy* are preoccupied with this question.

[57] I have here adopted Keith Ward's scheme in *The Development of Kant's View of Ethics* (Oxford: Basil Blackwell, 1972). See especially his conclusion, e.g.: "It is only within such a metaphysical context of demand, alienation and reconciliation that the doctrine of the categorical imperative emerges in its true complexity" (p. 173).

Morality is thus seen as a temporal process of the construction of new purposes by rational reflection and reciprocal response to other persons and changing situations.[58]

This is made yet clearer in Kant's essay on theodicies, the subject of the next section.

Kant and Theodicies

Kant, in his essay *On the Failure of All Attempted Philosophical Theodicies*,[59] addresses the question of complaints about the sorry state of the world, and he addresses them in what is a familiar religious setting. This essay, though not a commentary, is an analysis of arguments found in the *Book of Job*. Kant finds there the figure of the moral man, Job, who argues that the sufferings of life are senseless and cruel. Job's friends, when they finally have the courage to say anything to him, try to console him with arguments based upon notions about the arrangement of the moral universe that Job knows to be most likely. The arguments of Job's friends are what are called theodicies.

Kant defines theodicies as "defenses of the highest wisdom of the Creator against the complaints which reason makes by pointing to the existence of things which contradict wise purpose."[60] There are, according to Kant, but "three kinds of contradictions to purposefulness in the world out of which objections could be made to the wisdom of its Creator."[61] These objections are classified according to which of the attributes of the Creator the complaints are supposed to contradict. The Creator is said to be, (1) *holy* as a legislator, (2) *good* as a governor, and (3) *just* as a judge.[62]

Each of these is contradicted by a different kind of evil. Holiness is contradicted by moral evil (crime); goodness, by the sufferings of

---

[58]Ibid., p. 175.

[59]*Theodicee*, 6:119-39; Despland, pp. 283-97.

[60]Ibid., 6:121; Despland, p. 283.

[61]Ibid., 6:122; Despland, p. 284.

[62]Ibid., 6:123-24, Despland, p. 285.

rational beings (natural evil); and justice, by "the unbecoming disproportion between the impunity of the guilty and the gravity of their crimes."[63] To each of these complaints Kant constructs three separate theodicies designed to reconcile the contradictions implicit in the complaints. Kant does his best to argue God's case. The arguments he constructs (or reconstructs) he crystallizes from the *Book of Job*. Most of them are recognizable as the arguments of Eliphaz, Zophar, Bildad, and Elihu the theologian.[64] Each argument is designed to offer comfort and solace to those tormented by suffering in an uncanny world.

What Kant calls theodicies are really religio-metaphysical cosmologies, or teleological systems whose various authors and supporters assert a knowledge of the ultimate connection between the moral order of the universe and the natural order of it. This assertion would be much less objectionable were it not to be made so dogmatically, and were it not to claim knowledge of the intimate connections between each event and the supreme wisdom. Defenders of theodicy believe that the universe is a sort of immense natural-ethical-theological ecosystem in which each "offense" is followed by a punishment; each "pious act," a reward. And if we do not see these delicate balances it is because (a) our faculties are defective, (b) the reactions are delayed (even into an afterlife, or subsequent generations), (c) there are no evils to be seen—what we "call" evil is really some marvelous machination, or (d) because we ourselves have sinned and refuse to believe that punishment will follow. Kant deals with these arguments as one might expect.

These views must be rejected simply on the grounds that knowledge of the supreme wisdom and the workings of the universe writ large is beyond the power of the human understanding. Theodicies are the products of the same dialectical illusion that invents speculative metaphysical systems. They are simply the products of an

---

[63]Ibid.

[64]Cf. Nahum Glatzer, *The Dimensions of Job* (New York: Schocken Books, 1969). See Glatzer's introduction, pp. 37-39. Also, Robert Gordis, *The Book of God and Man* (Chicago: University of Chicago Press, 1965). See pp. 8, 155, 227, 366.

undisciplined theoretical reason. But however illusory they may be, they are embraced piously by many people as defenses against the encroachment of disturbing perceptions of the world around them. And to that extent they seem to provide some satisfactions to their advocates. They do provide certain incentives, therefore, which have some sort of utility.

Kant's concern is that the hopes produced by these theodicies are fragile and illusory, and that the incentives produced by them *displace* in practice moral incentives which are efficacious. The difference between the incentives produced by theodicies and those produced by reason's laws is the difference between unreliable ones and genuine trustworthy ones. But there is yet another problem with theodicies.

Uncritically held religious or metaphysical views produce in the believer a disposition to lie to himself. Once this disposition becomes firmly rooted it is nearly impossible to extirpate. In *Religion*, Kant puts the point graphically:

> It is expedient to believe too much rather than too little, on the ground that what we do over and above what we owe will at least do no harm and might even help. Upon this illusion, which makes dishonesty in religious confessions a basic principle (to which one subscribes the more easily since religion makes good every mistake, and hence of that dishonesty along with the rest), is based on the so-called maxim of certainty in matters of faith.[65]

He continues:

> *The hypocrite regards as a mere nothing* the danger arising from the dishonesty of his profession, *the violation* of his conscience, involved in proclaiming even before God that something is certain, when he is aware that, its nature being what it is, it cannot be asserted with unconditional assurance.[66]

---

[65] *Die Religion innerhalb der Grenzen der Blossen Vernunft* (1793), 6:338; *Religion within the Limits of Reason Alone*, translated by Theodore Greene and Hoyt Hudson (New York: Harper and Row, 1960), p. 176.

[66] *Religion*, 6:338-39; Greene, p. 177.

Kant's point, if one may be allowed the luxury of expanding it, is that apart from the fact that the theodicies fail to deliver what they promise, they make hypocrites of those who confess them. One who lies to himself about the order of the universe for the purpose of maintaining his respect for the moral law (if that is why he does it), commits a stupidity and a contradiction. He violates the law by telling a lie before the one who cannot be fooled (*der Herzenkuendiger*), and does damage to the very thing he tries to save.

This argument is precisely the one found in Kant's essay on theodicy:

> He who says to himself (or to God; in matters of religion this amounts to the same thing) that he *believes* something, without having perhaps given a single look at himself to ascertain whether he is indeed certain, or certain up to a point, of his conviction tells a *lie*, and his lie is not only the most frivolous one before the One who searches the heart, but it is also the most criminal one because it cuts under the ground of sincerity, the basis of every virtue.[67]

The problem with what Kant in this essay calls "such blind and exterior confessions" is that they can "bring about progressively, especially if they are the source of worldly advantages, a certain duplicity (*Falschheit*) in everyone's way of thinking."[68]

Doctrinal theodicies must be ruled out on two counts: (1) they are lies which reinforce duplicity, and are, as such, immoral; and (2) they undermine rather than support genuine moral incentives. Religious doctrines, no matter how piously embraced, cannot supplant morality or provide incentives to replace the moral ones. Complaints against the wise governance of the world cannot be defeated with arguments based on illusions. The only thing that can be said at this point is

> we are capable at least of a negative wisdom. We can understand the necessary limits of our reflections on the subjects which are beyond our reach. This can easily be

---

[67]*Theodicee*, 6:135-36; Despland, pp. 294-95.
[68]Ibid.

demonstrated and will put an end *once and for all* to the trial.[69]

The trial Kant mentions above is the one in which the pious comforters plea for God's cause.[70] The reason for the end to this trial is that the world, according to Kant,

> is always a closed book when we want to read the ultimate intention of God (which is always a moral one) from a world which is only an object of experience.[71]

What Kant learned was that, though theodicies cannot *prove* the harmony of the supreme wisdom with purpose in the world, neither can misology *disprove* it. Though human wisdom cannot reveal a wise Providence, such can, therefore, be critically postulated. Though experience cannot prove that virtue is rewarded and evil punished, neither can experience disprove it. In fact, Kant wanted to argue, we not only have a right to draw strength from a critically postulated Providence, we must, he suggests, postulate it to give a unity to our moral conduct.[72] This does not mean that we dogmatically assert it. It means that we use it as a heuristic concept, a regulative ideal. Though the hope one draws from such a postulate is an uncertain hope, it is better than none at all.

There is one certainty we can learn from these investigations, according to Kant. We must, to get through things, be honest with ourselves. He uses three different German words for this quality: "*Aufrichtigkeit*," "*Redlichkeit*," and "*Wahrhaftigkeit*."[73] Though they all capture virtually the same sentiment, they are translated differently. The first is "uprightness" or "straightforwardness." The second is "sincerity." The third is "truthfulness." None of these words has any of that flavor we have given "sincerity" these days—the flavor of a puppy earnestness. All have the sense of "candor" and "frankness" and "inner honesty."

---

[69]Ibid., 6:130; Despland, p. 290.

[70]Ibid., 6:132; Despland, p. 292.

[71]Ibid., 6:131; Despland, p. 291.

[72]*Religion*, 6:351; Greene, p. 189.

[73]*Theodicee*, 6:130; Despland, p. 290.

Kant's view finally is that respect for the moral law requires more than just its recognition. It requires an inner outlook that is conscientious and clear-sighted. This is a disposition which is gradually built as it is practiced. But in most men, Kant observed, it is sadly lacking. Kant discovered there is a universal tendency rooted firmly in human nature which is a radical insincerity, a duplicity which can be extirpated only with great discipline and hardship.

He added, therefore, to his conception of moral practice, which had previously contained the incentives of moral precepts, warnings about a natural dialectic, and pictures of moral pathology, a *new conception of moral discipline.* This discipline can be called "conscientiousness." It consists, Kant says, of two components:

> One can call sincerity the *formal conscience. Material conscience* is the concern never to say something which is wrong. The formal conscience consists in the consciousness of having maintained this concern in a given case.
>
> The formal conscience, which is the ground of all truthfulness, consists in the care that makes sure of what one believes and what one does not believe, and in the care never to state a conviction when one is not really certain of it.[74]

Conscientiousness is then the continued examination of conscience. Its role is to root out insincerity, which undermines moral practice just as surely as does any other practice which clouds the precepts of reason. It is the subjective ground of moral practice, just as the moral law is the objective ground of moral theory.

> There is something moving and edifying to the soul in the example of an upright character who has no trace of duplicity and dissimulation. And yet, especially in frank conversation, honesty is nothing but mere straightforwardness in one's way of thought. It is the least that one can ask from a man with a good character. It is hard to see then why this quality should receive such admiration. It must be, that of all qualities, honesty is the one which is furthest removed from human nature; sad observation,

---

[74]Ibid., 6:135; Despland, p. 294.

since all other qualities can have true worth only if they rest on this one![75]

The End of All Things[76]

In the preceding three sections I have introduced materials from three of Kant's later essays to present a description of the first two or three stages in the life of the moral person. Normally human life is conceived to be divisible into youth, adulthood, and old age. Kant's *Conjectural Beginnings of Human History* presents a detailed account of the emergence from "the womb of nature"—childhood—into youth. Generally this stage can be characterized as that in which the person first recognizes the moral demands made upon him. It is clearly an uncomfortable period in one's life, at least the way it is pictured in Kant's essay. This is because of the ambiguity with which the moral demands are felt.[77] The youth does not clearly distinguish between parochial demands coming from the immediate social setting and the categorical demands of the moral law. He is buffeted, therefore, between one conception of demand and another. The youth, since he is expelled from the garden of childhood, is unable to find his bearings.

If this is so, as it seems to be, then adulthood could be chiefly characterized as the alienation of a person from those demands—his recognition of the fact that his relationship to others is primarily antagonistic and that his efforts to create a world according to his own wishes will be frustrated in any social setting. He finds himself called "to achieve a rank among his fellows whom he cannot tolerate, but from whom he cannot withdraw."[78] He realizes that, though he cannot tolerate others who oppose him, he must nevertheless communicate his purposes to them, justify his conduct in open discussion, and make

---

[75]Ibid., 6:137, Despland, p. 296.

[76]*Ende.*

[77]Cf. John S. Dunne's *Time and Myth: A Meditation on Storytelling as an Explanation of Life and Death* (Notre Dame: University of Notre Dame Press, 1975). Dunne depicts the ambiguity of which I am writing in a much more poetic vein throughout his thoughtful book.

[78]*Idea*, 4:115; Beck, p. 15.

a life for himself in accordance with universal moral rules.

Adulthood is pictured, therefore, as that time in life during which a person's social interactions are animated by what appear to be contradictory demands—the demands of his own "calling" and the demands of society that his endeavors not frustrate the endeavors of others. William Butler Yeats has contrasted the period of youth, which he calls "the unfinished man and his despair" with the period of adulthood which he calls "the finished man among his enemies."[79] Yeats' description of adulthood is a nicely encapsulated version of Kantian descriptions of this period. An adult is "finished" when he is aware of his own projects. To say that he is among his enemies is to say that he recognizes that his own pursuits are often opposed to the pursuits of others.

The moral demand appears in adulthood as the requirement that the mature person strive to reconcile his pursuits with the legitimate pursuits of others. Adulthood is then the attempt of the person who recognizes the realities of antagonism and alienation to reconcile these oppositions. Old age can be thought of as the eventual reconciliation of these oppositions. Kant's descriptions of this period in life can be extrapolated from his discussion of various conceptions of what Kant calls "the last day." Eschatological theories occupy a central place in Kant's discussion of *The End of All Things*.[80] Their relevance to an attempt to complete a moral biography should become evident.

But to make it clear just how eschatological notions figure in the conception of old age it would help to recall Socrates' discussion with Cephalus in Book 1 of Plato's *Republic*[81]

Cephalus, it will be remembered, is an aged businessman in the position of surveying his own life with the purpose of deciding whether or not he has left important things undone. Socrates engages him in discussion in order to learn from the aged "who have preceded us on a

---

[79]William Butler Yeats, *A Vision* (New York: Collier, 1966), p. 220. See especially his poem entitled *Dialogue Between Self and Soul*.

[80]*Ende*, 6:4ll; Beck, p. 69.

[81]I cite from Paul Shorey's translation of *Republic* in *Plato: Collected Dialogues*, edited by Hamilton and Cairns, (Princeton: Princeton University Press, 1978), pp. 575-844.

road on which we too, it may be, must sometime fare—what it is like."
Socrates asks:

> Is it rough and hard-going or easy and pleasant to travel?
> And so now I would fain learn of you what you think of this
> thing, now that your time has come to it, the thing that the
> poets call "the threshold of old age." Is it a hard part of life
> to bear or what report have you to make of it?[82]

As one would expect, Cephalus explains that there are many
things an old man misses about his youth and his adulthood as well as
many things from which he is happy to be free. But primarily,
Cephalus says,

> when a man begins to realize that he is going to die, he is
> filled with apprehensions and concern about matters that
> before did not occur to him. The tales that are told of the
> world below and how the men who have done wrong here
> must pay the penalty there, though he may have laughed
> them down hitherto, then begin to torture his soul with the
> doubt that there may be some truth in them. And apart from
> that the man himself either from the weakness of old age or
> possibly as being now nearer to the things beyond has a
> somewhat clearer view of them. Be that as it may, he is filled
> with doubt, surmises, and alarms and begins to reckon up
> and consider whether he has ever wronged anyone. Now he
> to whom the ledger of his life shows an account of many evil
> deeds starts up even from his dreams like a child again and
> again in a fright and his days are haunted by anticipations of
> worse to come. But on him who is conscious of no wrong
> that he has done a sweet hope ever attends and a goodly, to
> be nurse of his old age, as Pindar too says.[83]

The question of old age is whether it is impossible for a person who
has lived a long life to reconcile himself to what he knows to have been
his own life conduct. And this is the topic of Kant's *The End of All
Things*. Kant's view in this essay is that the last day must, for

---

[82]*Republic*, 328e.

[83]Ibid., 330e-331a.

practically moral purposes, be conceived as *a day of judgment*.[84] Though no sense can really be made of "eternity" nor of an "end of time," people, Kant says, from all cultures have imagined a time after all time during which they will be repaid for the deeds they have done in their lives. This "time after all time" has usually been conceived either as eternal bliss or eternal misery, though some sects have claimed that all persons are redeemed rather than damned.

There are two systems, Kant says, which have characterized men's thinking about eschatological matters.[85] The first he calls the "Unitarian system," in accordance with which salvation is awarded to all men who are "purified by means of more or less lengthy penances." The second Kant calls the "Dualistic system," in accordance with which some "select ones" are awarded salvation and all the rest "eternal damnation."[86] Kant's appraisal of the two systems is interesting.

The unitarian system, according to Kant, has the least difficulties from the theoretical point of view, because it recognizes the fact that ultimate judgments of the worth of persons cannot be made by rational creatures. Kant puts the point as follows:

> For what person knows himself and others so thoroughly as to decide whether, in the allseeing eye of a Judge of the world, one man has an advantage in every respect over another in his inner moral worth, if he separates from the causes of his presumably well-conducted life everything which is called the wages of success, for example, his congenitally amiable temperament, the naturally greater vigor of his higher powers (of his understanding and reason so as to check his impulses), and the occasions when chance spared him many temptations which befall others. And if he does separate all this from his true character (as he necessarily must subtract it in order to evaluate this thing properly, since he cannot credit it as being a fortunate gift of

---

[84] *Ende*, 6:412; Beck, p. 70.

[85] Ibid., 6:413; Beck, p. 71.

[86] Ibid.

his own merit), who will then decide, I say, whether one man
has advantage of more moral worth over another? And may
it not be perhaps as stupid a self-conceit in this superficial
self-knowledge to pass any judgment in his own favor
concerning his own moral worth (and deserved fate) as it
would be to pass any judgment on others?[87]

The unitarian system rewards all, since judgments of inner moral
worth cannot be accurately made, and since a system which damns all
equally "could not be tenable since thereunder there would be no
justification for their having been created in the first place" it follows
that the unitarian system does less violence to our hopes than the other
systems.[88]

However, from the moral point of view, the unitarian system must
be rejected for the reason that it might lull men to sleep with its
assurances of reward, regardless of their life conduct. From the
morally practical point of view one must adopt as a regulative
principle the Dualistic system. The point is not that the dualistic
system is the true one. All such eschatalogical systems are speculative
and therefore unknowable. The point is that the adoption of the
Dualistic system produces a pressure to improve present conduct.
Kant argues the point as follows:

We must judge that those principles of our behavior in life
which we have found governing in us (be they good or evil)
until its end, will also continue to prevail after death, and we
have not the slightest reason to assume an alteration of them
in that future. Therefore, we would also have to anticipate
consequences commensurate with this fault or that virtue
for all eternity under the dominion of the good or evil
principle; in this sense it is wise then to so act *as if* another
life, and the moral state in which we terminate the present
one along with its consequences upon entering another one,
are unchangeable. From a practical point of view, therefore,
the system to be embraced will have to be the Dualistic one,

---

[87]Ibid., 6:414; Beck, p. 72.
[88]Ibid.

especially since the Unitarian system seems to be too much lulled asleep in complacent security; still we do not want to determine which of the two merits preference in a theoretical and purely speculative sense.[89]

In old age, as in the other stages of life, conceptions of the end of all things serve, at best, as practical pictures of the whole of life. We are pressured by them to conceive of our lives as moral unities on the basis of which reflective judgments concerning our present purposes and projects can be made. Old age, if it has any distinctive characteristic, is that time in life when the conceptions of moral unity are paramount. We survey our lives with the purpose of arriving at some judgment about our moral dispositions, as Kant calls them. "In these circumstances," Kant writes,

> then nothing else remains for reason except to visualize a variation that progresses into the infinite (in time) within the perpetual progression toward the ultimate purpose in connection with which its *disposition* endures and is itself constant, a disposition which is not mutable like that progression of a phenomenon, but is rather something supersensible and is, consequently, not fluctuating in time. The rule for the practical use of reason according to this Idea, therefore, intends to express nothing more than that we must take our maxims as if, in all its changes from good to better which proceed into the infinite, our moral state, with respect to this disposition (the *homo noumenon*, "whose change takes place in heaven") would not be subjected to temporal change.[90]

The Moral Biography in Retrospect

We may conclude from the previous sketch of the moral biography several interesting things. It is evident that a whole life is lived toward rationally constructed goals, and that these goals may be altered as they are gradually approached. It is evident, as well, that the course of

---

[89]Ibid., 6:414-15; Beck, p. 73.

[90]Ibid., 6:419; Beck, pp. 77-78.

a life is not the function of purely biological processes. One's life consists of much more than merely biological growth or development. Kant's sketches of life-courses are really significant because of the absence of the notions of natural or supernatural ends. The teleology which animates them is a teleology of freedom. This is depicted, in his works, as the gradual "insinuation" of reason (the various ends of freedom) into the life of an individual. What is clear is that the ends of freedom do not run parallel to the ends of nature. Indeed, many rational ends run counter to the ends of nature. That is why Kant describes the passage from childhood to adolescence as the discovery of our powers over nature.

The rational construction of ends for a course of human life consists then of the attempt on the part of an individual to build for himself what Kant repeatedly calls "character." It is evident from his sketches of character that the limitations on the construction of selves are not primarily natural limitations. They are, instead, the limitations that are self-imposed, limitations that are a function of an agent's own unwillingness to free himself from certain natural ways of thinking about his own life.

If he supposes, for example, that he cannot alter or avoid what is currently being called "the mid-life crisis," then he will probably have to endure it just in the sense that popular conceptions of that "crisis" will animate, indeed "determine," his passage through "it." If he believes that he has no control over the associative processes of thought, then his thinking will most probably reflect just such processes. If, however, he believes (is convinced) that he has control over the course of his own life, he will discover, probably to his surprise, that he does have such control. Kant's point is that rational conceptions of life—conceptions guided by moral laws—have efficacy only to the extent that we allow them to have such efficacy in our own lives. The refusal to admit such is also a refusal to live rationally. We are condemned to various determinisms unless we renounce them in favor of our own life-plans.

Conclusion

Final Remarks
on Kant's Conception
of Moral Practice

In an effort to bring together the most important of the themes which have been dealt with in the body of this study, these closing remarks will focus upon four themes: (1) moral consciousness as a non-habitual attitude, the maintenance of which requires a discipline of reason; (2) freedom and honesty as the supreme practical values; (3) tensions between Kant's conception of moral practice and political life; (4) the need for incentives other than the purely moral one to reinforce the moral disposition.

Moral Consciousness as a Non-Habitual Attitude

Moral consciousness as a way of thinking about ourselves and others is a consciousness in which the moral aspects of our experience are not simply discovered, but are, in a real sense, created. Before we are able to treat ourselves and others as *ends*, we must first be able to think of ourselves and others as ends. It is clear, I think, from what I have presented in the preceding chapters, that Kant regarded the development of this ability to be the most important single achievement of a moral agent. It is clear, as well, that without the adoption of this way of thinking, acts, however good they may otherwise be, cannot claim any *moral worth*. It is the consciousness which conditions the acts which gives them their morality. The morality of acts, thus, depends upon the dispositions which animate or motivate them. This Kant made clear in the *Groundwork*. The problem, then, for the person who attempts to live a moral life is the problem of how to revolutionize his attitudes or his dispositions.

The revolution of attitudes, a "Copernican revolution," appears to take place in *single explosive acts*. The agent, disgusted with himself because of his imprisonment in habits which he acquired gradually during his youth, at one or several points in his life renounces his previous way of living. This amounts to a renunciation of the powers that had gradually imprisoned him in certain natural ways of thinking. It amounts as well to an affirmation of his freedom from the chains of habit. The revolution, however, as I hope to have shown, is brought about by a criticism which clarifies the field of consciousness so that the moral law can be grasped in its purity. Kant's view is that once the moral law is grasped clearly it directly determines the will. What this means is that it is allowed to replace the natural inclinations as the principal guide in the moral agent's life. The moral law in its purity is, according to Kant, sublime. It is that in contrast with which all else is small. It causes, therefore, in the moral agent a feeling which Kant calls "respect." This feeling is the feeling of being free from the natural inclinations which had previously corrupted the agent's will.

But as Kant pictures the revolution in attitudes, the initial resolve to respect the moral law, to obey it, is still not enough. One's resolve is constantly in danger of being re-corrupted by natural inclination, which, if left unchecked, gradually erodes one's commitments to moral principles and eventually imprisons one again in the routines of natural consciousness. One's life then crystallizes into repetitive efforts to win happiness by attempting to satisfy the impetuous demands of natural desires. Consequently, Kant insists upon the necessity for a continuous discipline, an arduous struggle, to maintain the initial resolve. Habits apparently cannot be destroyed once and for all. They must be mastered. And this mastery is the most difficult aspect of moral practice.

The difficulty is that the mastery of habits can never become habitual, it can never become easy and natural. As a result moral agents can never become morally perfect. At best they are able continually to progress toward moral betterment under the constant tutelage of the moral law. Moral betterment comes to mean, for Kant, the gradual ability to make use of reason in conduct. This ability develops only with practice and experience in the world. An agent begins more and more to appreciate the extent to which he is free to do his duties even in the face of powerful counter-tendencies. But since morality can never become habitual, constant vigilance is required to maintain a confidence in the freedom of oneself from nature's habits. The moral attitude, which is an attitude of freedom, must be monitored carefully. The monitoring agent is conscience.

Freedom and Honesty as Supreme Moral Values

It is clear that if moral attitudes constantly struggle with habits, then they are reciprocally the attempts of moral agents to establish freedom in an agent's way of thinking. Morality, as Kant describes it, is a spontaneity of reason under moral laws. One must be free to adopt moral attitudes and then free to realize moral goals in conduct. Freedom is, therefore, a supreme moral value. However, as Kant has shown, and as I hope to have made clear, human beings constantly deny their freedom by lying to themselves about their duties, especially when natural circumstances make doing their duties difficult.

Consequently, freedom cannot flourish in the life of an agent who is not honest with himself. It cannot be recommended to others if we are not honest with them as well. Perhaps freedom and honesty are more closely related in Kant's moral philosophy than they might at first glance seem to be. If moral attitudes must precede action in order to give it moral worth, the gradual undermining of these attitudes must be quickly detected. This cannot be done if one is not honest with oneself about one's own convictions and especially about the subtle ways in which one is able to fool oneself into thinking that some overpowering circumstances "free" one from one's duties. Morality cannot survive in a climate of rationalization. This much is quite clear.

Honesty is the straightforward recognition of the fact that we rationalize our duties continually, and it is the effort to destroy such rationalizations each time they arise. Honesty is part of moral discipline.

Kant is aware of the fact, however, that people are not always, or even usually, honest with themselves or with others. They have, Kant discovered, a tendency to be reticent about their own beliefs, especially the open confession of them. This reticence is simply the lack of candor. Even when we tell the truth, we do not always tell the whole truth. We have learned through bitter experience that to do so might bring us to ruin in our professions or in our social lives. But this is a fault for which we can at least be forgiven. In social settings everyone conceals at least part of what he genuinely believes. And it is clear from Kant's texts that such concealment is a part of what we call common decency. But there is a still subtler and more damaging kind of dishonesty which is inexcusable. This is radical evil.

If reticence is the unwillingness to express the whole truth, then radical evil is the deliberate expression of a falsehood, the deliberate concealment of our true aims and purposes. Radical evil is, for Kant, the lie which undermines morality completely. Reticence is but human frailty expressing itself in a lack of candor. Radical evil is something much worse. It is moral worthlessness.

Moral worthlessness is, clearly, the very opposite of a moral disposition. As such it represents an almost total bondage of an agent to powerful and natural ways of thinking about himself and others. Typically, the morally worthless person makes excuses for not doing his duties, excuses which he himself knows to be lies. The advantages that have accrued to him over the course of his worthless life have gradually, but certainly, taken possession of his powers of thinking freely, and of thinking honestly. He is, therefore, totally irresponsible. But this picture of him is a picture of the totally worthless person. It happens, fortunately, that though we are all worthless in various degrees, we are not all totally worthless. We all have, according to Kant, this subtle tendency to lie, and it is against this tendency which we must constantly struggle. This struggle is, in substance, the essence of morality in practice. The struggle is for an honesty which sees to it that our freedom is not destroyed, and that our moral outlooks are maintained with integrity.

In chapter two sketches were presented of three character types representative of typical character defects—the pedant, the empiricist, and the mystic. Each of these characters represents moral failure attributable to different kinds of dishonesty. The pedant conceals from himself the core of morality which is a freedom from trivial routines. The empiricist excuses himself from duties by saying that he should not be expected to do what others do not do. He has discovered that people do not fulfill their obligations and concludes that trying to fulfill them is a foolish undertaking because it is too difficult to swim upstream. And the mystic lies to himself by claiming that he is exempt from obligations by virtue of his intimate relationship with the deity. Since he is a favorite in God's house he does not need to win favor by doing his chores.

So it is clear, I think, that both freedom and honesty, for Kant, are supreme moral values. Without them both, moral attitudes are corrupted at their very basis. A lack of conviction in these values inevitably brings, according to Kant, the collapse of morality. But there are further complications that must be addressed. Being free and being honest is difficult enough in the best of circumstances, as Kant seems to picture it. How much more difficult must it be then in a modern society?

Tensions Between Moral and Political Life

If thinking freely and thinking honestly are supreme moral values, as evidently Kant believes them to be, it is clear that in modern societies, especially, such practices are made increasingly more difficult. There is a close connection between thinking freely and honestly, and expressing thoughts freely and honestly. Freedom and honesty of thought does not seem to survive well in our atmosphere of universal suspicion and mistrust. One finds these days (as perhaps in all times) that the frank confession of one's convictions almost guarantees, except in very special settings (about which more will be said later), serious misunderstanding. It is as if open avowals of our convictions in the arena of public discourse, an arena which seems to be more suitable for the exchanging of ideologies rather than doubts we may have about this and that, is regarded as a sort of foolishness which guarantees the failure of our short-term purposes.

Our intentions seem somehow to lose their meaning when joined with others in large coalitions, simply because others implicitly presume without prior adequate discussions that would make various intentions clear, that our goals are the same as theirs. Thus, there is, it seems to me, a kind of paradox similar to the one Plato identifies in his *Republic*. Men of good will are almost inevitably misunderstood in political settings. For them to be understood adequately would require that which cannot be expected: a whole society of persons of good will.

The moral person is faced with a profound dilemma. Either he acts in the full knowledge of the fact that his actions will be misunderstood and consequently perverted in the political arena, or he is forced to ignore the ultimate consequences of his moral actions. In the first case he is blamed for his lack of concern, or for his self-righteousness. In the second he is viewed as a naif, a simpleton who does not understand the machinations of *Realpolitik*. In either case he will acquire the peculiar stigmata of someone who does not care about social welfare or of someone who knows nothing about it.

Kant has said of the moral person that he appears to the world as one not wise after the manner of men. His straightforwardness is strangely out of place. He appears to live in a different world because, in some significant sense, he does. The moral agent, as Kant pictures him, is one whose eyes and thoughts are directed toward the world as it ought to be, not the world as it is.

But however ineffective he may be in the immense sphere of modern politics, he is, nevertheless, as Kant pictures him, a man who commands the respect of those who really know him. Ludwig Ernst Borowski, one of Kant's close friends, has given us an interesting picture of Kant himself, a picture which illustrates at least part of what has been suggested above. "My sketch of Kant," Borowski writes,

> would be very unlike if a certain kindly, comfortable picture of Kant did not come before the eyes of my reader. He was certainly not one who failed to recognize his own worth, nor one who tolerated willful neglect; but all the same he was an exceptionally good-natured, unpretentious man. He had a hundred traits which had to appeal to anyone who knows anything of human merit. They made him attractive in society, sought for by all and agreeable to everyone. I used to call him a *childish man*. Just yesterday I used the word

"childishness" with reference to him. "Right," cried my old friend Scheffner, who knew our philosopher very well indeed; "the word 'childishness' expresses the whole Kant!" Or, to sum him up in another word: humanity. Humanity in the full sense of this now so frequently used word but best defined by Kant himself, could be ascribed to Kant in a high degree. Not only his naturally good disposition (a certain lovable simplicity), but also his acquired maxims and principles led him to humanity. He remained true to it until his death. Here among us there was probably not a single enemy of Kant's; he certainly had more friends than ever a man in his position had.[1]

Borowski is quoted not to elegize Kant so much as to emphasize the characterization of him as a "childish man" with "a certain lovable simplicity" which won the respect and love of those who knew him.

What seems equally clear is that this "childish man" did not seem to have had many astounding successes in the politics of his day. He was not as *immediately* influential as was Rousseau or perhaps even Hume. This leads to an important point.

Morality, as Kant pictures it (even as he exemplifies it), does not *seem* to be politically effective only because its effects are subtle and long lasting. Historians are more capable of estimating the effects of a Napoleon on his own time, because his actions were pronounced and immediately felt by the entire Western world. The quiet work of a moral person cannot so easily be evaluated, because, it seems, the consequences are radiated by example and by legend and they do not seem to be easily detected. The effects and affects of the moral person appear chiefly in the lives of those who come to know him either through the inspirations of his example, or through his oral and written teachings. Kant's own description of a moral person is

---

[1]Ludwig Ernst Borowski, *Darstellung des Lebens und Charakters Immanuel Kants* (1804), in *Immanuel Kant, Ein Lebensbild*, ed. Hermann Schwarz (Halle: Meiner, 1907), pp. 68-69. Quoted from L. W. Beck's translation in his *Early German Philosophy: Kant and His Predecessors* (Cambridge: Harvard University Press, 1969), pp. 437-38.

evidence of this. He writes, in his *Beobachtungen über das Gefühl des Schönen und Erhabenen:*

The person whose feeling leans toward melancholy is called melancholy, not because he broods in morose heaviness of heart robbed of all the joys of life, but because, if his emotional reactions were to be enhanced beyond a certain measure or were to be misdirected for any reasons, they would more easily tend towards that condition than to any other. He has a special *feeling for the sublime.* Even beauty, for which he also has a feeling, must not merely charm but also move him, inasmuch as it fills him at the same time with admiration. The enjoyment of pleasures is more serious, but on that account no less enjoyable. All emotions of the sublime contain more enchantment for him than all deceitful enticings of the beautiful. His well-being will be closer to contentment than to gaiety. *He is steadfast.* For that reason he regulates his emotions by principles. The more general the principle of regulation, the broader the high feeling which comprises the lower one within itself, the less these emotions yield to unsteadiness and change. . . . The person of melancholy frame of mind cares little for what others think, what they consider good or true; he trusts entirely to his own insight. Since his grounds of motivation take on the nature of principles he is not easily brought to other ideas; occasionally his steadfastness degenerates even into willfulness. He looks upon the change of fashions with indifference and upon glamour with contempt. Friendship is sublime and is therefore agreeable to his temperament. . . . Affable conversation is beautiful, thoughtful silence is sublime. He's a good keeper of his secrets as well as of those of others. Veracity is sublime; he hates lies and pretense. He has a high regard for the dignity of human nature. He esteems himself and regards any man as a creature deserving of respect. He will endure no depraved submissiveness and breathes freedom in a noble breast. He abominates all chains, from the gilded ones worn at court to the heavy irons of the galley-slave. He is a severe judge of himself and of

others and not rarely is disgusted with himself as well as with
the world.[2]

Here is a portrait of a person who has learned to master his
dispositions, and to do so he has had to adopt a studied indifference to
the things that excite most people. It is this attitude to the things of the
world which at once makes him a moral exemplar and a sort of political outcast, one who is frequently misunderstood and unappreciated
by those who do not know him well. And it is this which makes clear
the tensions between moral and modern political life.

These tensions are apparent to the moral person. Kant recognizes
that they must be confronted. Indeed, Kant himself advocated and
practiced political involvement, and was himself misunderstood.
Kant's political experiences were not, to be sure, as frightful as were
Plato's at Syracuse, but the last ten to fifteen years of his life were spent
in attempts to address serious political issues and to understand the
frustrations produced by political involvements. In his late essays, and
even in the third *Critique*, the method for dealing with them is made
clear.

The Need for Additional Incentives

The fact that the actions of moral persons are not immediately
apparent in the political arena appears to them and to others as an
acute form of injustice. Moral persons must suffer calamities along
with all the rest. It seems that their good conduct and their moral
dispositions do not win for them any special dispensations in the
visible world. As Job complained, the wicked prosper and the deeds of
moral persons go unrewarded as well as unnoticed. There does not
seem, therefore, to be any harmony between the ends of moral life and
the natural purposes of the world. Morality does seem to be
condemned to survive in a larger moral vacuum.

Without the sense that moral actions add up to something,
advance the *Summum Bonum*, the incentives that inspire moral agents
to act morally begin to corrode. This Kant has made clear throughout

---

[2]*Beobachtungen über das Gefühl des Schönen und Erhabenen*, quoted
from Paul A. Schilpp's *Kant's Pre-Critical Ethics* (Evanston: Northwestern
University Press, 1960), p. 4.

his third *Critique* and in his *Religion*. Reason, according to Kant, is not satisfied with less than harmony. Consequently the moral agent is compelled by reason to construct the notion of the ultimate harmony of the intelligible and the natural worlds. He is compelled to see in nature the symbols of that harmony, symbols which generate in him feelings which further reinforce his moral attitudes. These feelings are caused by his reflections on his self-constructed cosmos, a cosmos in which goodness is rewarded and evil is ultimately destroyed.

Without these rational constructions his moral efforts are attenuated, his resolves are dissipated, and he is in danger of losing his moral outlook. So from the subjectively practical standpoint the moral agent must necessarily erect an ethico-religious perspective to embrace his moral attitudes, but he must not make the mistake of reifying his own constructions. He must, instead, maintain himself with respect to them in a relationship of what Kant calls a "doubtful faith."

This strategy, *and it is a strategy*, prevents the agent from viewing himself as one who acts for narrow and apparently fruitless purposes. The lesson here is that *moral tactics* cannot be maintained in the absence of an overarching *ethico-religious strategy*. But since the ultimate effects of his tactics are unknown to him, both because he does not know the various long-term consequences of his acts and because he cannot be objectively certain that his strategy is the correct one, he lives constantly in a state of hopeful and doubtful expectation.

He must draw strength, then, from his own resources and from his interactions with other moral persons. And what this means, to make what would otherwise be a very long discourse very short, is that he is not really as self-sufficient as he might originally have thought himself to be.

One begins Kant's works with impressions about the self-sufficiency of the moral individual, gathered largely from his critical writings, especially his *Groundwork*. One ends by seeing that the moral individual cannot survive as such. He must place his life, ultimately, in the hands of an ethico-religious community in which he is understood and appreciated. Kantian moral philosophy is, after all is said about it, not really a secular humanism as it has so often been made out to be. It lives squarely in the middle of traditional religious conceptions of human life. And it is this which has been responsible for the fact that it has survived the assaults of the past two centuries of philosophic thought.

Selected Bibliography

Since the secondary literature on Kant is immense, I have presented a selected bibliography of books and articles that have been particularly useful to me; ones that are relatively recent; and ones readily available to readers of English. I have also included a list of readily available English translations of Kant's works.

Kant's Works

Kant, Immanuel. *Immanuel Kants Werke*. Edited by Ernst Cassirer. Eleven Volumes. Berlin: Bruno Cassirer, 1912-1922. (All references in the text of this essay are to Cassirer's edition of Kant's work. Titles are abbreviated and are followed by the volume number, page, translator's last name, and page number of translation.)

———— *Anthropology*. Translated by Mary J. Gregor. The Hague: Martinus Nijhoff, 1974.

———— *Critique of Judgment*. Translated by James Creed Meredith. Oxford: Oxford University Press, 1952.

————*Critique of Practical Reason*. Translated by Lewis White Beck. New York: Bobbs-Merrill, 1956.

————*Critique of Pure Reason*. Translated by Norman Kemp Smith. London: MacMillan, 1973.

————*Education*. Translated by A. Churton. Ann Arbor, Michigan: The University of Michigan Press, 1960.

————*Foundations of the Metaphysics of Morals* and *What is Enlightenment?* Translated by Lewis White Beck. New York: Bobbs-Merrill, 1959.

————*Inaugural Dissertation of 1770*. Translated by William J. Eckoff. New York: AMS Press, Inc., 1970.

————*Kant's Lectures on Philosophical Theology*. Translated by Allen W. Wood and Gertrude M. Clark. Ithaca: Cornell University Press, 1978.

_____ *Kant's Political Writings*. Edited by Hans Reiss and translated by H. B. Nisbet. London: Cambridge University Press, 1970.

_____ *Lectures on Ethics*. Translated by Louis Infield. Indianapolis: Hackett Pub. Co., 1980.

_____ *Logic*. Translated by Robert S. Hartman and Wolfgang Schwarz. New York: Bobbs-Merrill, 1974.

_____ *Metaphysical Foundations of Natural Science*. Translated by James Ellington. New York: Bobbs-Merrill, 1970.

_____ *Metaphysics of Morals*. Part 1: *The Metaphysical Elements of Justice*. Translated by John Ladd. New York: Bobbs-Merrill, 1965. Part 2: *The Metaphysical Principles of Virtue*. Translated by James Ellington. New York: Bobbs-Merrill, 1964.

_____ *Observations on the Feeling of the Beautiful and the Sublime*. Translated by John T. Goldthwait. Berkeley: University of California Press,1965.

_____ *On History*. Essays edited and translated by Lewis White Beck. New York: Bobbs-Merrill, 1963.

_____ *On the Old Saw: That May be Right in Theory but it Won't Work in Practice*. Translated by E. B. Ashton. Philadelphia: University of Pennsylvania Press, 1973.

_____ *Philosophical Correspondence*, 1759-99. Translated by Arnulf Zweig. Chicago: University of Chicago Press, 1967.

_____ *Prolegomena to Any Future Metaphysics*. Translated by P. Carus. LaSalle,Illinois: The Open Court Publishing Co., 1965.

_____ *Religion within the Limits of Reason Alone*. Translated by Theodore M. Greene and Hoyt H. Hudson. New York: Harper and Row Torchbooks, 1960.

_____ *Universal Natural History and Theory of the Heavens*. Translated by W. Hastie. Ann Arbor, Michigan: The University of Michigan Press, 1969.

Articles

Allison, Henry E. "Kant's 'Transcendental Humanism'." *The Monist* 55 (1971): 182.

Alstom, William P. "Feelings." *Philosophical Review* 78 (1969): 3.

Auxter, Thomas. "The Unimportance of Kant's Highest Good." *Journal of the History of Philosophy* 17:2 (April, 1979): 121.

Barker, S. F. "Appearing and Appearances in Kant," *The Monist* 51 (1967): 426.

Baumer, Wilean H. "Kant on Cosmological Arguments." *The Monist* 51 (1967): 519.

Beck, Lewis White. "Kant's Theory of Definition." *Philosophical Review* 65 (1956): 179.

_____. "Nicolai Hartmann's Criticism of Kant's Theory of Knowledge." *Philosophy and Phenomenological Research* 2 (1941-42): 472.

Bennett, Jonathan. "Strawson on Kant." *Philosophical Review* 77 (1968): 340.

Benson, John. "Emotion and Expression." *Philosophical Review* 76 (1967): 335.

Bird, G. H. "The Necessity of Kant." *Mind* 68 (1959): 389.

Brandt, Richard B. "The Emotive Theory of Ethics." *Philosophical Review* 59 (1950): 305.

Brown, Stuart M., Jr. "Has Kant a Philosophy of Law?" *Philosophical Review* 71 (1962).

Clark, Gordon H. & Schrader, George A. "Some Questions on Kant." *The Review of Metaphysics* 5 (1951-52): 473.

Cleobury, F. H. "Post-Kantian Idealism and Modern Analysis." *Mind* 61 (1952): 359.

Collins, James. "A Kantian Critique of the God-is-Dead Theme." *The Monist* 51 (1967): 536.

Curtler, Mercer. "What Kant Might Say to Hare." *Mind* 80 (1971): 295.

Dryer, D. P. "Concept of Existence in Kant." *The Monist* 50 (1966): 17.

Fackenheim, Emil. "Kant and Radical Evil." *University of Toronto Quarterly* 23 1953-54).

French, Stanley G. "Kant's Constitutive-Regulative Distinction." *The Monist* 51 (1967): 623

Friedman, Laurence. "Kant's Theory of Time." *The Review of Metaphysics* 7 (1953-54): 379.

Geach, P. J. "The Perils of Pauline." *Review of Metaphysics* 23 (1969-70): 287.

Genova, A. C. "Kant's Complex Problem of Reflective Judgment." *Review of Metaphysics* 23 (1969-70): 452.

Gordon, L. M. "Conventional Expressions of Emotion." *Mind* 78 (1969): 35.

Gotlind, E. "Mr. Hampshire on the Analogy of Feeling." *Mind* 63 (1954): 519.

Gram, M. S. "Kant's First Antinomy." *The Monist* 51 (1967): 499.

Green, O. H. "The Expression of Emotion." *Mind* 79 (1970): 551.

Gregor, M. J. "Laws of Freedom: A Study of Kant's Method of Applying the Categorical Imperative in the *Metaphysik der Sitten*." Mind 75 (1966): 297.

Hampshire, S. "The Analogy of Feeling." *Mind* 61 (1952): 1.

Hartshorne, Charles. "Kant's Refutation Still Not Convincing: A Reply." *The Monist* 52 (1968): 314.

Henrich, Dieter. "The Proof-Structure of Kant's Transcendental Deduction." *Review of Metaphysics* 22 (1968-69): 640.

MacBeath, A. M. "Kant on Moral Feeling." *Kant-Studien* 64 (1973): 283.

McCloskey, Mary A. "Pleasure." *Mind* 80 (1971): 542.

Milmed, Bella K. "Kant and Current Philosophical Issues." *Philosophical Review* 74 (1965).

_____ "Possible Experience and Recent Interpretations of Kant." *The Monist* 51 (1967): 442.

Mischel, Theodore. "Kant and the Possibility of a Science of Psychology." *The Monist* 51 (1967): 599.

Moore, A. "The Emotive Theory and Rational Methods in Moral Controversy." *Mind* 60 (1951): 233.

Murphy, Jeffrie G. "Kant's Concept of a Right Action." *The Monist* 51 (1967): 574.

Nahm, Milton C. " 'Sublimity' and the 'Moral Law'." *Kant-Studien* 50 (1958-59): 502.

Parsons, Charles. "Infinity and Kant's Conception of the Possibility of Experience." *Philosophical Review* 73 (1964): 182.

Peirce, C. S. "The Fixation of Belief." In *The Enduring Questions*. Second Edition. Edited by Melvin Rader. New York: Holt, Rinehart and Winston, 1976.

Rech, Andrew J. "Insight and the Eros of the Mind." *The Review of Metaphysics* 12 (1958-59): 97.

Rees, D. A. "Kant, Bayle, and Indifferentism." *Philosophical Review* 63 (1954): 592.

Rotenstreich, Nathan. "Kant's Dialectic." *The Review of Metaphysics* 7 (1953-54): 389.

Schrader, George A., Jr. "The Thing in Itself in Kantian Philosophy," *The Review of Metaphysics* 2 (1948-49): 30.

_____ "The Transcendental Ideality and Empirical Reality of Kant's Space and Time." *The Review of Metaphysics* 4 (1950-51): 507.

Schwarzschild, Steven S. "The Tenability of Herman Cohen's Construction of the Self." *Journal of the History of Philosophy* 13 (July 1975).

Sellars, Wilfred. "Kant's Views on Sensibility and Understanding." *The Monist* 51 (1967): 463.

Silber, John R. "Kant's Conception of the Highest Good as Immanent & Transcendent." *Philosophical Review* 68 (1959): 469.

Smith, John E. "Hegel's Critique of Kant." *Review of Metaphysics* 26 (1972-73): 438.

———— "Kant, Paton and Beck: A Critical Study." *The Review of Metaphysics* 3 (1949-1950): 229.

Stevenson, Charles L. "The Emotive Concept of Ethics and Its Cognitive Implications." *Philosophical Review* 59 (1950): 291.

Thomas, S. B. "Jesus and Kant." *Mind* 79 (1970): 188.

Thomas, V. "Ethical Disagreement and the Emotive Theory of Values." *Mind* 60 (1951): 205.

Vuillemin, Jules. "*La Théorie Kantienne de l'espace à la lumière de la théorie des groupes de transformations.*" *The Monist* 51 (1967): 332.

Walsh, W. H. "Kant on the Perception of Time." *The Monist* 51 (1967): 376.

Ward, K. "The Ascription of Experiences," *Mind* 79 (1970): 415.

Weldon, J. D. "Introduction to Kant's *Critique of Pure Reason.*" *Philosophical Review* 56 (1947): 44.

Wick, Warner A. "Moral Problems, Moral Philosophy, and Metaethics." *Philosophical Review* 62 (1953): 3.

Zemach, E. M. "Seeing, Seeing, and Feeling." *Review of Metaphysics* 23 (1969-1970): 3.

Books

Bainton, Roland H. *The Reformation of the Sixteenth Century.* Boston: Beacon Press, 1956.

Barth, Karl. *Protestant Thought from Rousseau to Ritschl.* London: SCM Press, 1959.

Beck, Lewis White. *A Commentary on Kant's Critique of Practical Reason.* Chicago: University of Chicago Press, 1961.

———— *Early German Philosophy: Kant and His Predecessors.* Cambridge: Harvard University Press, 1969.

————, ed. *Kant Studies Today.* LaSalle, Illinois: Open Court Library of Philosophy, 1969.

Benjamin, Walter. *The Origin of German Tragic Drama.* Translated by John Osborne. London: NLB, 1977.

Bennett, Jonathan. *Kant's Dialectic.* London: Cambridge University Press, 1974.

Broad, C. D. *Kant: An Introduction.* Edited by C. Levy. London: Cambridge University Press, 1978.

Buber, Martin. *Good and Evil: Two Interpretations.* Translated by Ronald Gregor Smith. New York: Charles Scribner's Sons, 1953.

Cassirer, Ernst. *Rousseau, Kant, and Goethe.* New York: Harper and Row Torchbooks, 1963.

———— *The Philosophy of the Enlightenment*. Translated by Fritz C. A. Koelln and James P. Pettegrove. Boston: Beacon Press, 1955.

Cassirer, H. W. *A Commentary on Kant's Critique of Judgment*. New York: Barnes and Noble, Inc., 1938.

Collins, James. *The Emergence of Philosophy of Religion*. New Haven: Yale University Press, 1967.

Despland, Michel. *Kant on History and Religion*, with a translation of Kant's "On the Failure of All Attempted Philosophical Theodicies." Montreal and London: McGill-Queen's University Press, 1973.

Donagan, Alan. *The Theory of Morality*. Chicago: University of Chicago Press, 1977.

Dunne, John S. *Time and Myth*. South Bend, Indiana: University of Notre Dame Press, 1973.

Feinberg, Joel, and Gross, Hyman. *Philosophy of Law*. Belmont, California: Dickenson Publishing Co., 1975.

Frankena, William K. *Ethics*. Englewood Cliffs, New Jersey: Prentice-Hall, Inc., 1973.

Galston, William A. *Kant and the Problem of History*. Chicago: University of Chicago Press, 1975.

Gewirth, Alan. *Reason and Morality*. Chicago: University of Chicago Press, 1978.

Glatzer, Nahum. *The Dimensions of Job*. New York: Schocken Books, 1969.

Goldmann, Lucien. *Immanuel Kant*. Translated by Robert Black. London: NLB, 1971.

Gordis, Robert. *The Book of God and Man*. Contains a new translation of the *Book of Job*. Chicago: University of Chicago Press, 1965.

Gregor, Mary J. *Laws of Freedom*. Oxford: Basil Blackwell, 1963.

Hampshire, Stuart. *Two Theories of Morality*. Oxford: Oxford University Press, 1977.

Hordern, William. *Living by Grace*. Philadelphia: Wadsworth, 1977.

Hume, David. *A Treatise of Human Nature*. Edited by L. A. Selby-Bigge. Oxford: Oxford University Press, 1958.

Jaspers, Karl. *Kant*. New York: Harcourt, Brace and World, A Harvest Book, 1962.

Johnson, Samuel. "Vision of Theodore, Hermit of Teneriffe." *The Works of Samuel Johnson*. A New Edition in Twelve Volumes. Vol. 2. London: Printed by Luke Hanfard, 1806.

Körner, S. *Kant*. Baltimore: Penguin Books, 1955.

Kroner, Richard. *Kant's Weltanschauung*. Translated by John E. Smith. Chicago: University of Chicago Press, 1956.

McFarland, J. D. *Kant's Concept of Teleology*. Edinburg: Edinburg University Press, 1970.

Medina, Angel. *Reflection, Time, and the Novel*. London: Routledge and Kegan Paul, 1979.

Murdoch, Iris. *The Sovereignty of Good*, New York: Schocken Books, 1971.

Paton, H. J. *The Categorical Imperative: A Study in Kant's Moral Philosophy*. New York: Harper and Row, 1967.

Plato. *The Collected Dialogues of Plato*. Edited by Edith Hamilton and Huntington Cairns. Princeton: Princeton University Press, 1961.

Schilpp, Paul A. *Kant's Pre-Critical Ethics*. Evanston: Northwestern University Press, 1960.

Ward, Keith. *The Development of Kant's View of Ethics*. Oxford: Basil Blackwell, 1972.

Willey, Thomas E. *Back to Kant: The Revival of Kantianism in German Social and Historical Thought, 1860-1914*. Detroit: Wayne State University Press, 1978.

Wolff, Robert Paul. *The Autonomy of Reason: A Commentary on Kant's Groundwork of the Metaphysics of Morals*. New York: Harper and Row, 1973.

Wood, Alan W. *Kant's Moral Religion*. Ithaca: Cornell University Press, 1970.

_____ *Kant's Rational Theology*. Ithaca: Cornell University Press, 1978.

Yeats, W. B. *A Vision*. New York: Collier, 1966.

_____ *The Collected Poems of W. B. Yeats*. New York: Macmillan, 1956.

INDEX

Adam and Eve, 104
abstraction, 110
"Achtung," 49
adulthood, stage of, 137
aesthetic/religious dimensions of
  morality, 13
agents, moral, 2
antagonism, social, 141
Aristotle, 6
artifice of philosophizing, 29
artless finality, 122*n*
attitude, component for, 2;
  empirically conditioned, 4
author of nature, 95

bad habits, 71
bad manners, 111
bad person, naively, 21;
  self-consciously, 21
Baier, Kurt, 10
beautiful/sublime the, 91
Benjamin, Walter, 104
"Beurteilung," 85*n*
Book of Job, 146
Borowski, Ludwig Ernst, 164-65
Buber, Martin, 21*n*

Cassirer, H. W., 93*n*
categorical imperative, 16, 18, 39, 54
Cephalus, 153-54
character, 2;
  defective, 2, 45, 78*n*
"common maxims of the world," 53
common run of men, the, 20*n*
common human reason, 4, 11*n*;
  compass of, 13, 16, 40
conscience, 17, 81;
  formal, 151,
  as an inner judge, 84;
  material, 151
conscientiousness, 154
Copernican revolution, 109, 113, 160
correct practice, 72
criminal, 17
criticism, 38, 40;
  philosophical, 14

Critique, the first, 90;
  the second, 90;
  The Critique of Judgment, 90
culture, 70

Descartes, 36
Despland, Michel, 7
determinant judgments, 94
devils, 75, 76
discipline, 58, 69, 90
dispositions, moral, 1, 2
dogmatic, 89
Don Quixote, 36
Donagan, Alan, 7, 24
Dunne, John S., 37*n*, 152*n*

ectypal worlds, 96-97
empirical moral viewpoints, 28
empirical psychologists, 57
empiricism of practical reason, 85
empiricist theory, 7, 98
enlightened egoist, 76
Enlightenment, 74
eschatological systems, 155
explosion, 80

favorites of God, 88, 163
fanatics, 88, 89
feeling, 42
Fontenelle, Bernard, 12
formulae, misuse of, 64
Frankena, 44*n*
freedom, 161-62
free teleology, 129
French Revolution, the, 24

Galston, William, 7, 114
genius, 89;
  extravagancies of, 125
Genova, A. C., analyses of the third
  Critique, 7, 87*n*, 91*n*, 94*n*, 95*n*
Glatzer, Nahum, 147*n*
good citizen, 75
good heart, 21
goodwill, 1-2, 102
graces, 20